THE
DRAWING
BOOK
FOR
KIDS

365 Daily Things
to Draw, Step by Step

Published by Turner Publishing Company

The Drawing Book for Kids: 365 Daily Things to Draw, Step by Step

Woo! Jr. Kids Activities Founder: Wendy Piersall

Art Director/Instructions Writted and Illustrated by: Lilia Garvin

Cover Illustration: Michael Koch | Sleeping Troll Studios www.sleepingtroll.com

Interior Illustration: Avinash Saini

ISBN 9781642506389 (paperback)

How to Use This Book!

All you need is a pencil, eraser, and a piece of paper!

Follow each drawing diagram step by step:

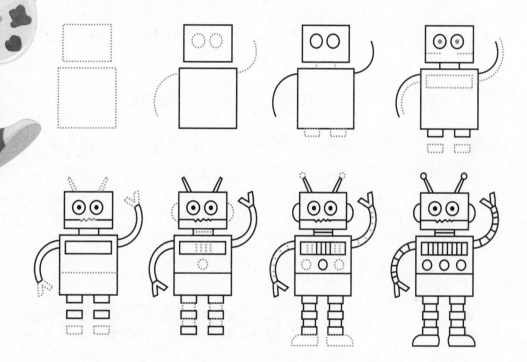

Tips:

Draw lightly at first, because you might need to erase some lines as you work.

Add details according to the diagrams, but don't worry about being perfect! Artists frequently make mistakes – they just find ways to make their mistakes look interesting.

Don't worry if your drawings don't turn out the way you want them to. Just keep practicing! Sometimes drawing the same thing just a few times will help.

Once you've finished your drawing in pencil you can trace it with a black fineliner pen and color or paint it to your liking.

You can draw a new item or character every day for 365 days – or use your creativity to combine multiple drawings into an entire scene.

Turn the page for some cool composition ideas!

Put Drawings together to create full scenes!

- Underwater Scene -

#14
Crab

#16
Starfish

#18
Stingray

#282
Mermaid

#21
Hammerhead Shark

#23
White Shark

#24
Whale

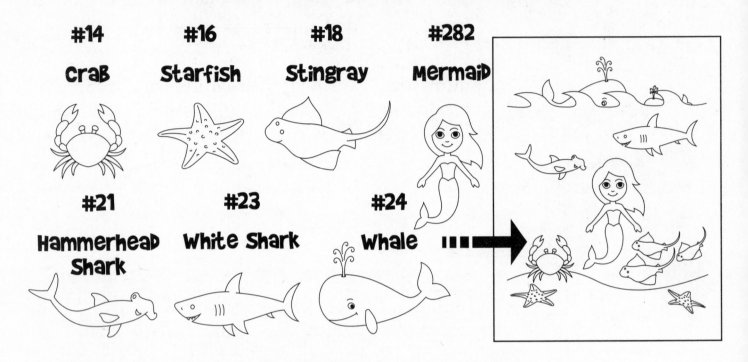

- Fishing Scene -

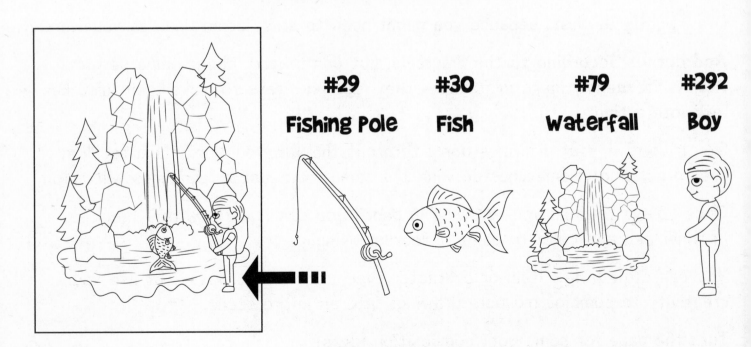

#29
Fishing Pole

#30
Fish

#79
Waterfall

#292
Boy

Put Drawings together to create full scenes!

– Outer Space Scene –

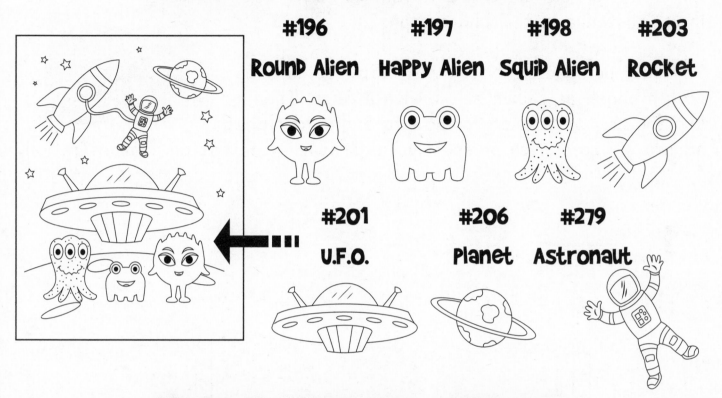

#196 Round Alien

#197 Happy Alien

#198 Squid Alien

#203 Rocket

#201 U.F.O.

#206 Planet

#279 Astronaut

– Flying Fairies Scene –

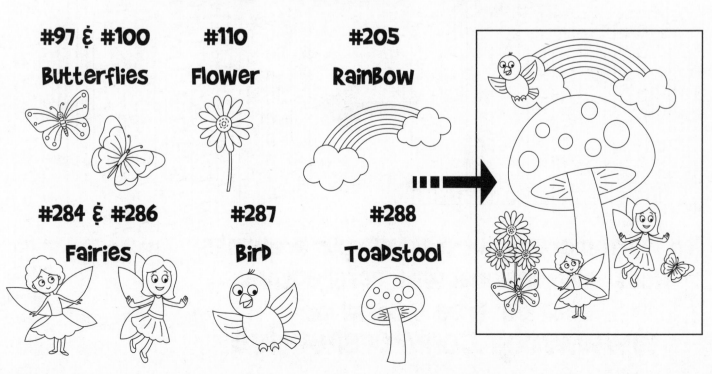

#97 & #100 Butterflies

#110 Flower

#205 Rainbow

#284 & #286 Fairies

#287 Bird

#288 Toadstool

ADD Perspective to your Drawings By using the vanishing Point and a Perspective grid!

The "vanishing point" is a point on the horizon in which a set of parallel lines appear to converge into a single point.
For example, railroad tracks appear to converge in the distance in this photograph:

To use a perspective grid, lightly draw guide lines with a pencil as shown below with a ruler. Then use the grid as a guide for how to angle your lines accurately to convey perspective as shown in the bottom demonstration.

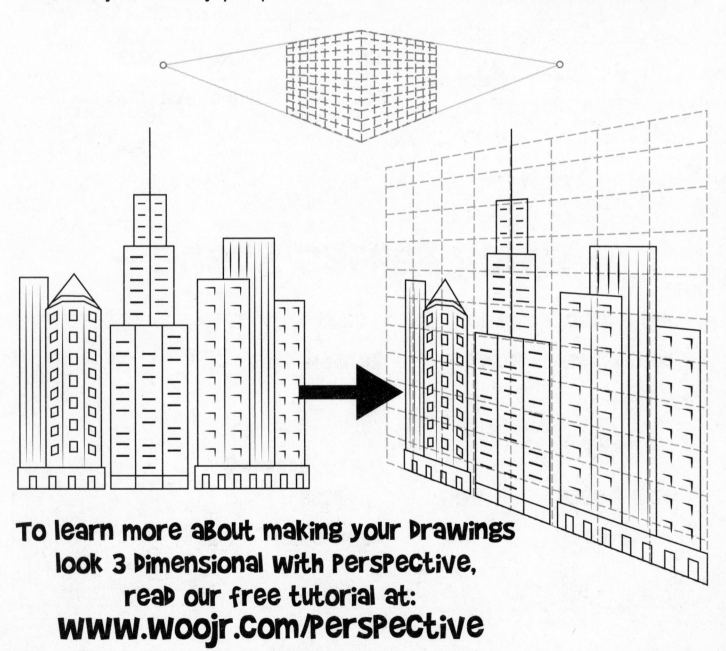

To learn more aBout making your Drawings look 3 Dimensional With Perspective, read our free tutorial at:
www.woojr.com/Perspective

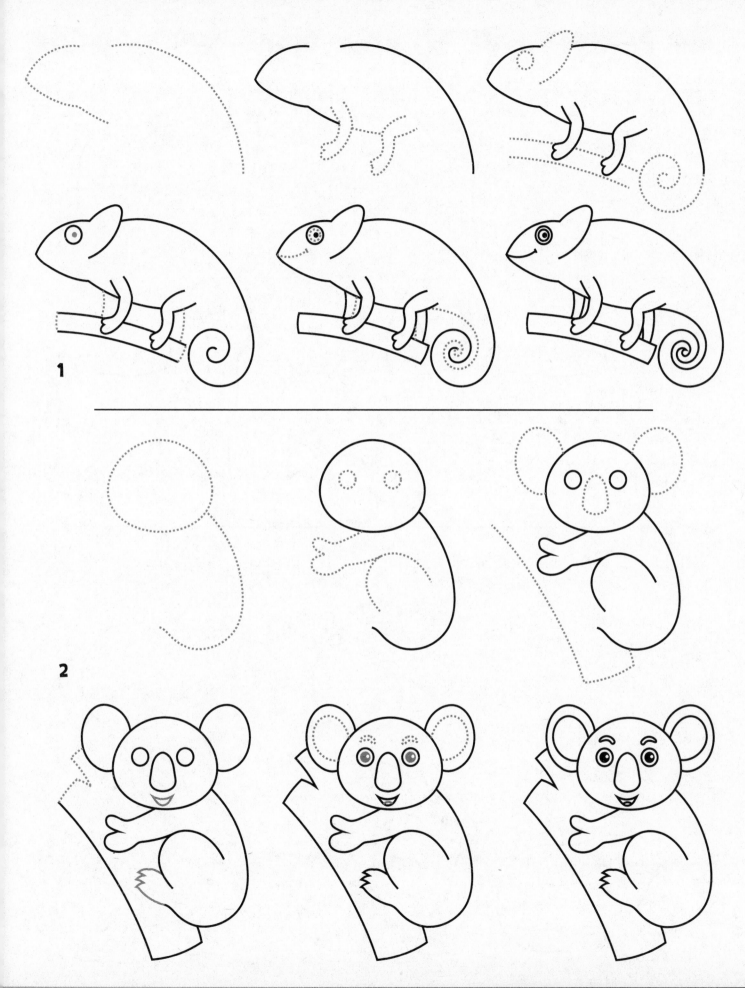

1

2

3

4

5

6

7

8

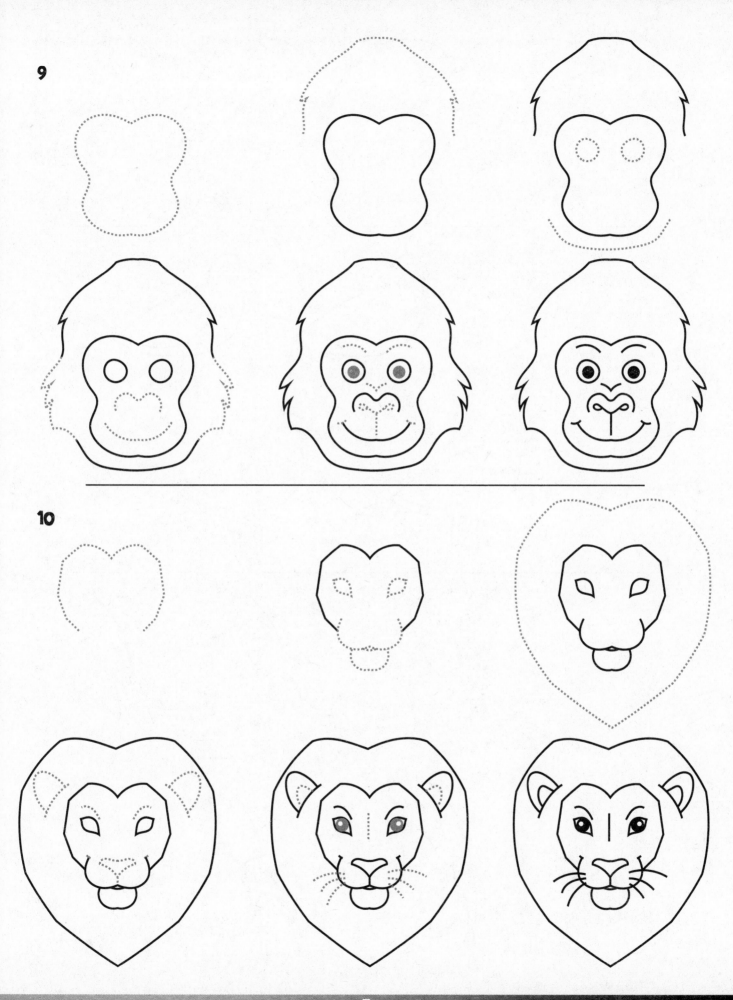

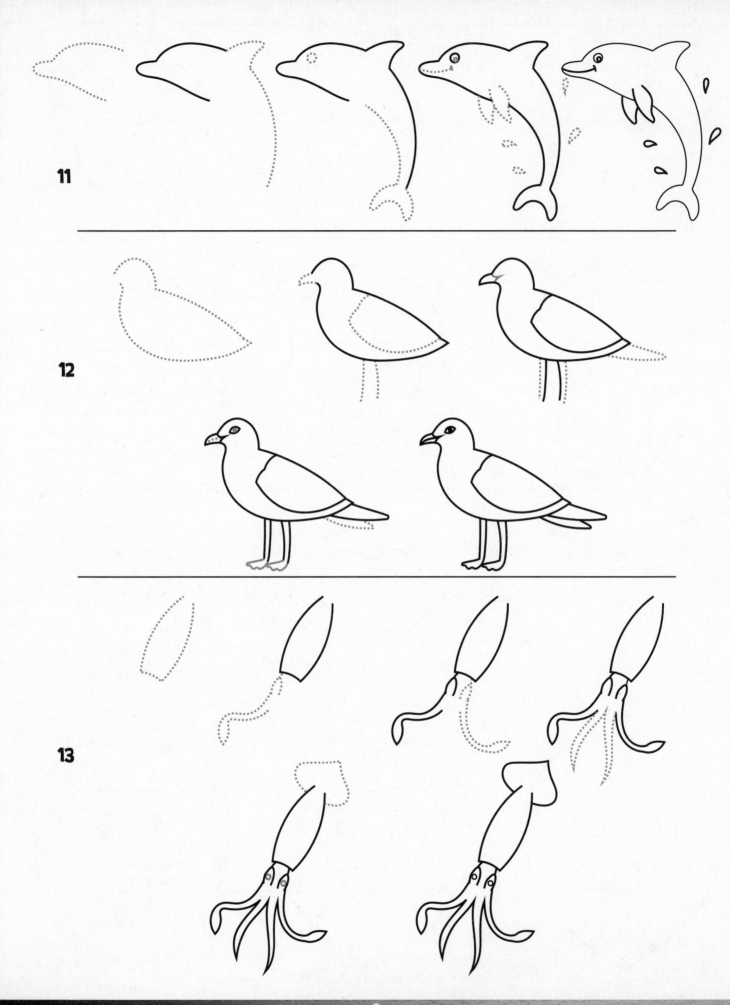

11

12

13

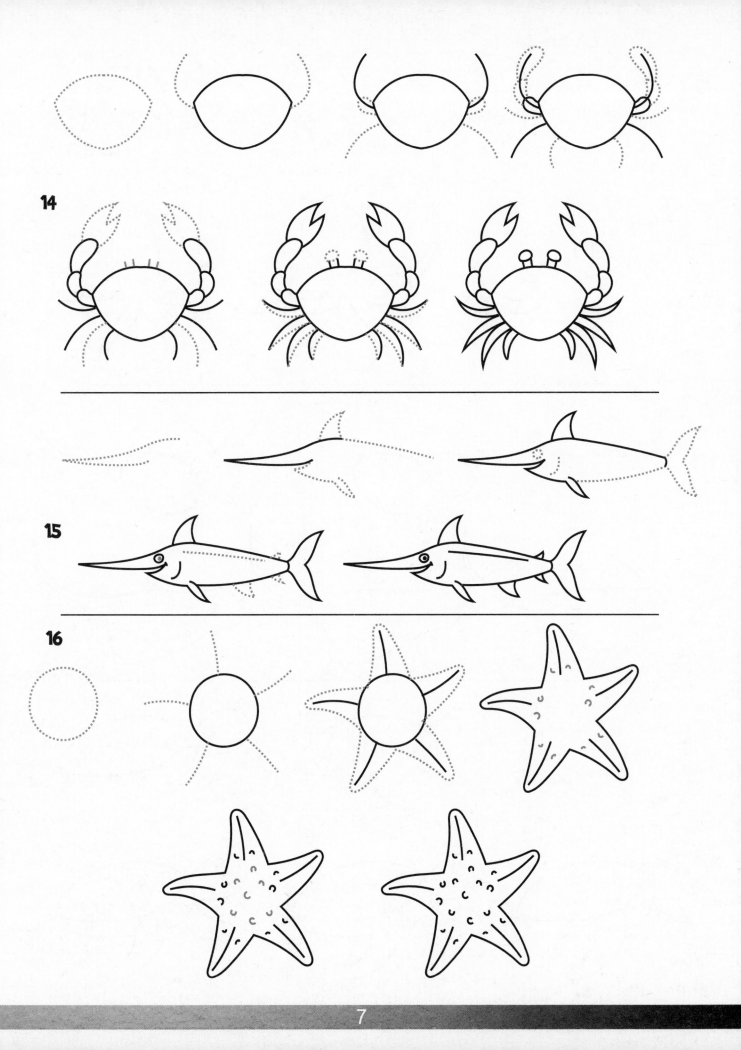

14

15

16

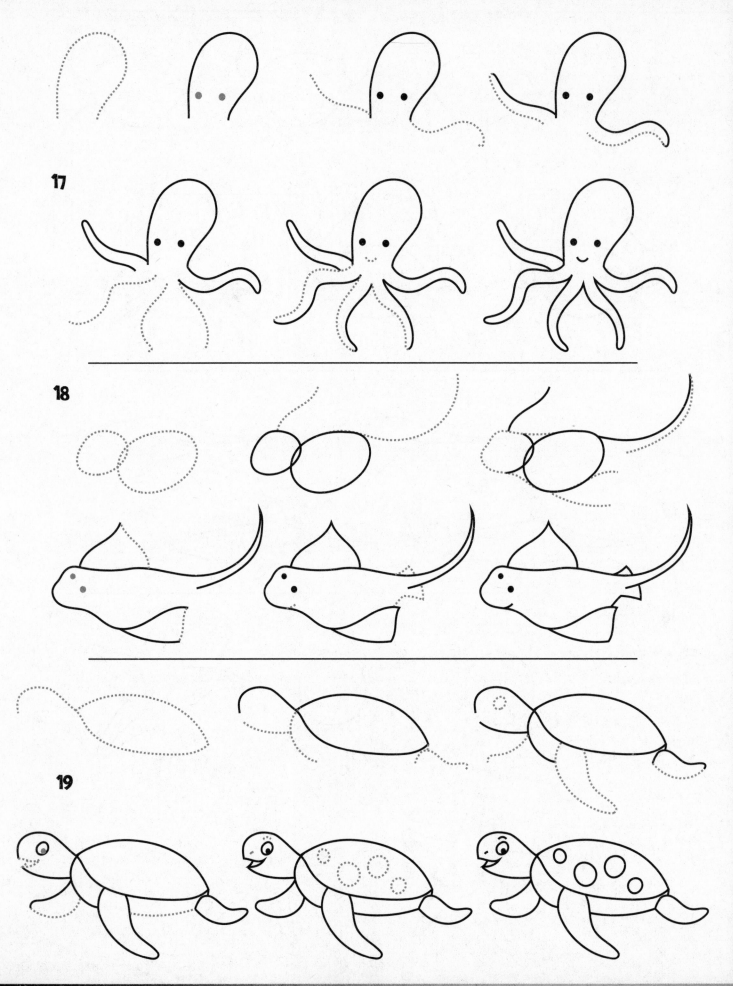

17

18

19

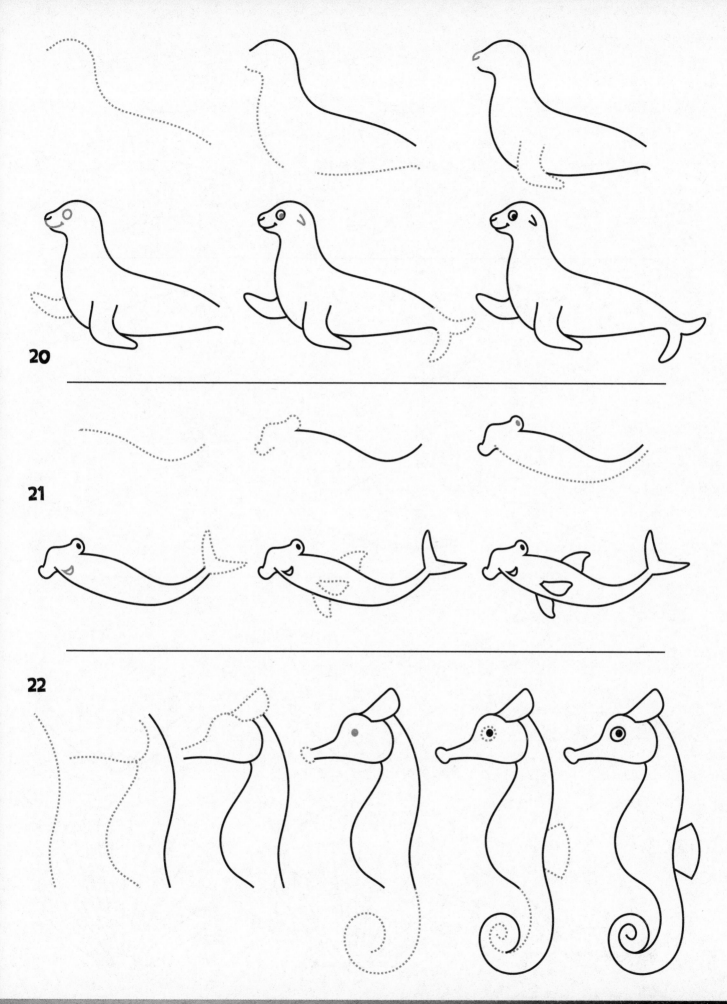

20

21

22

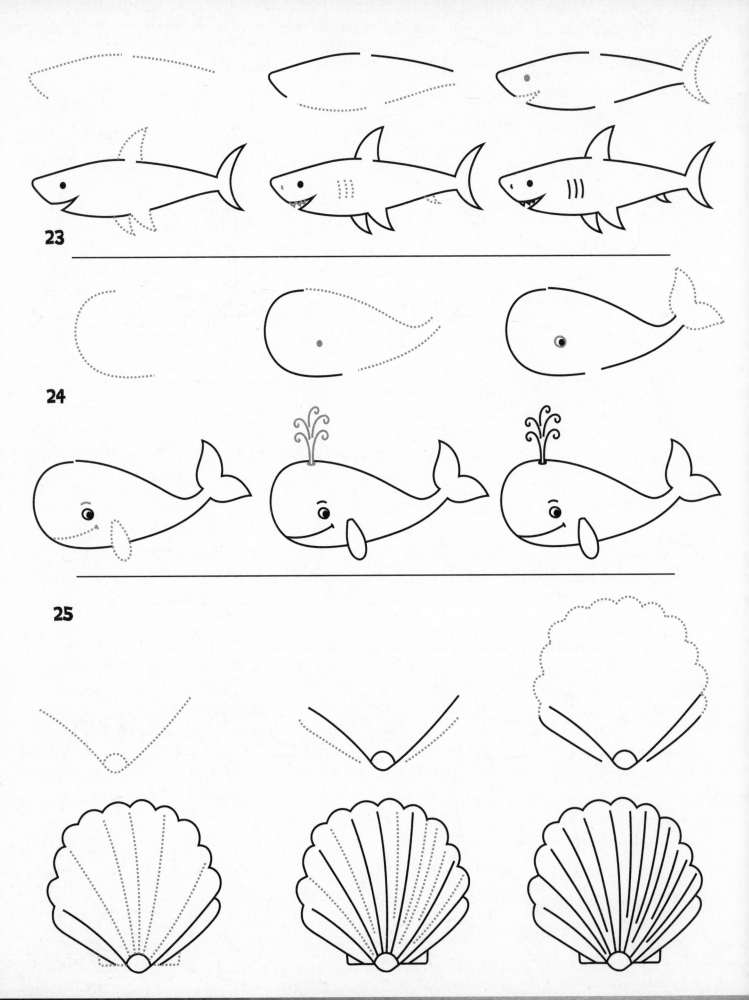

23

24

25

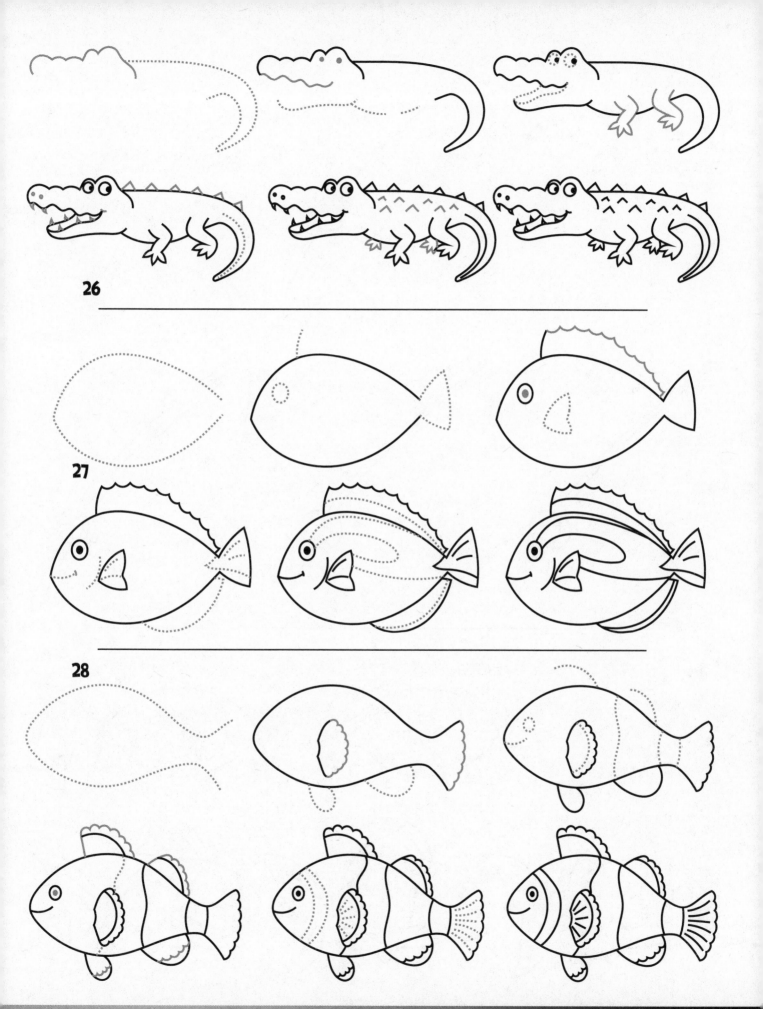

26

27

28

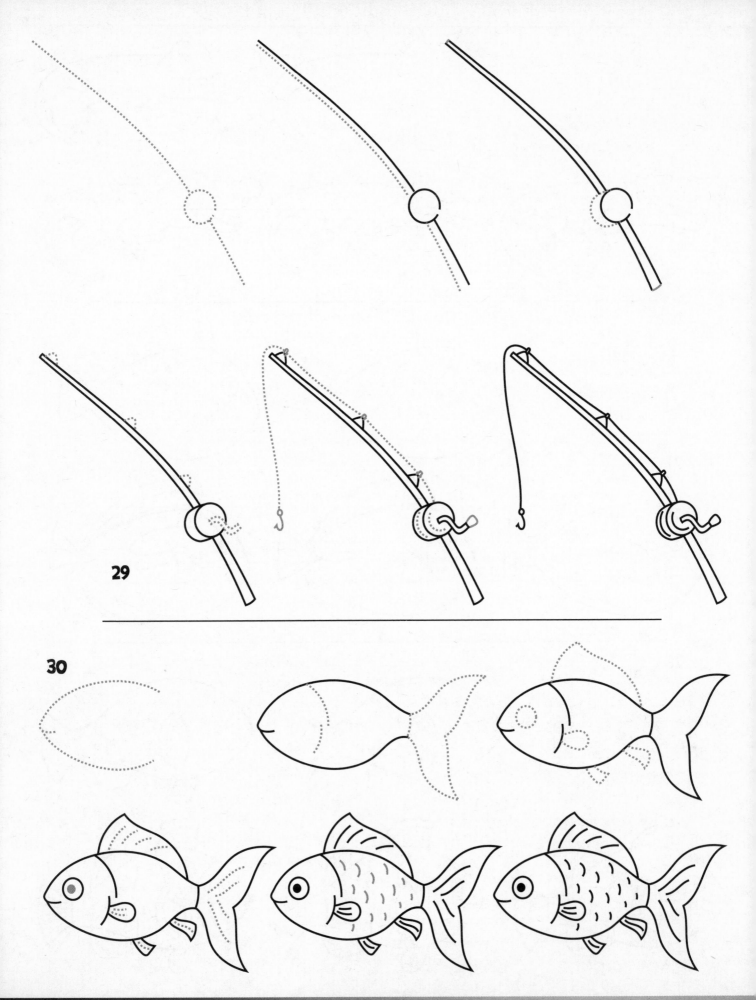

29

30

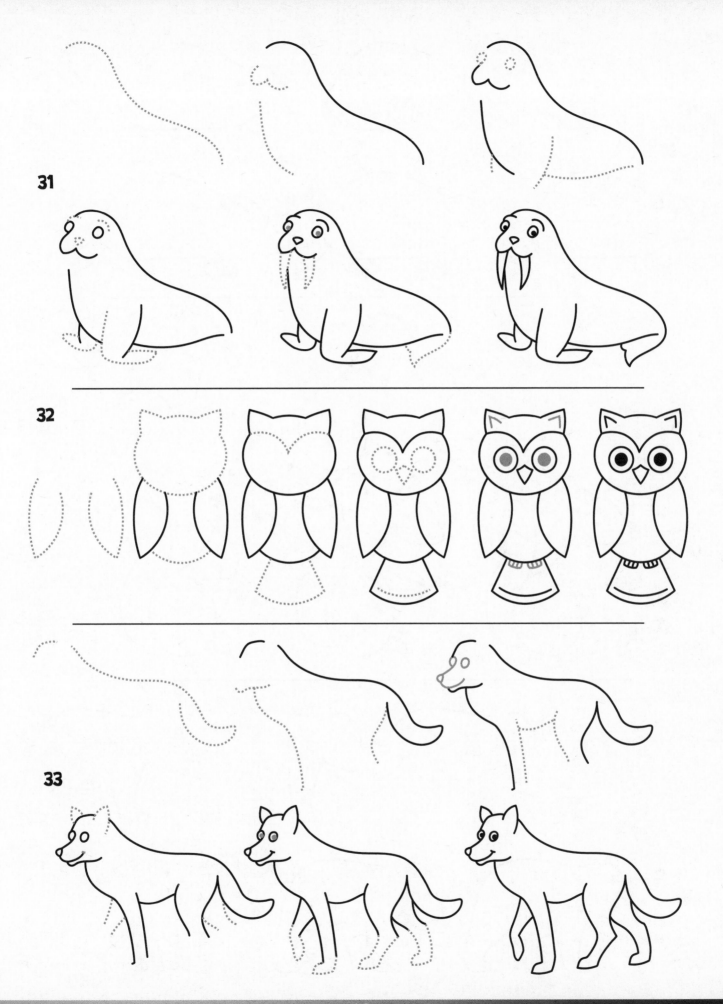

31

32

33

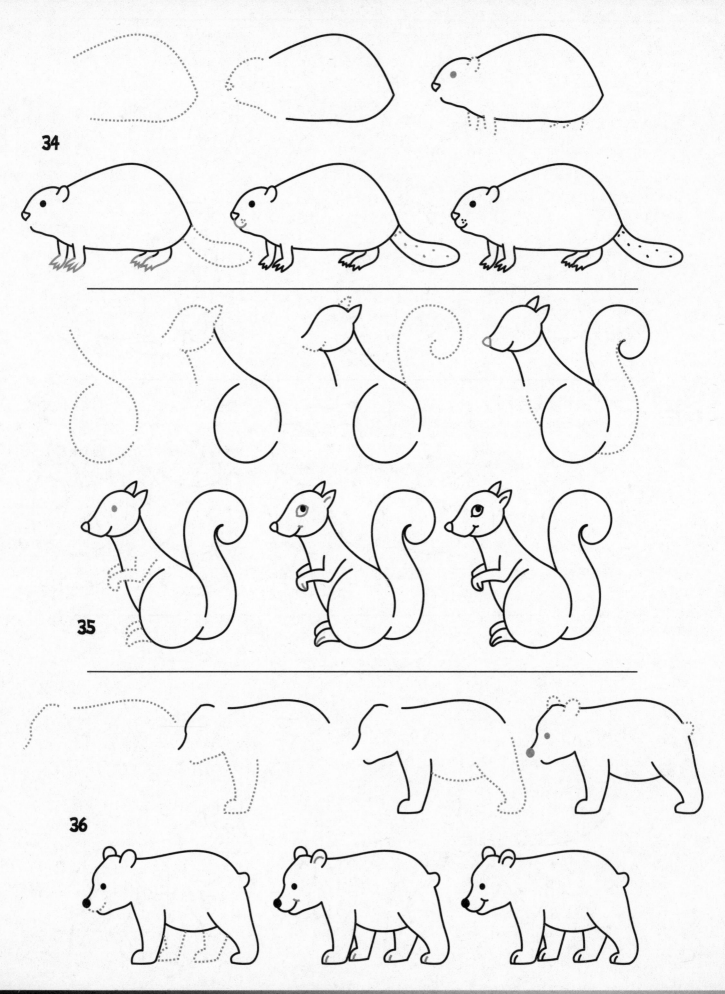

34

35

36

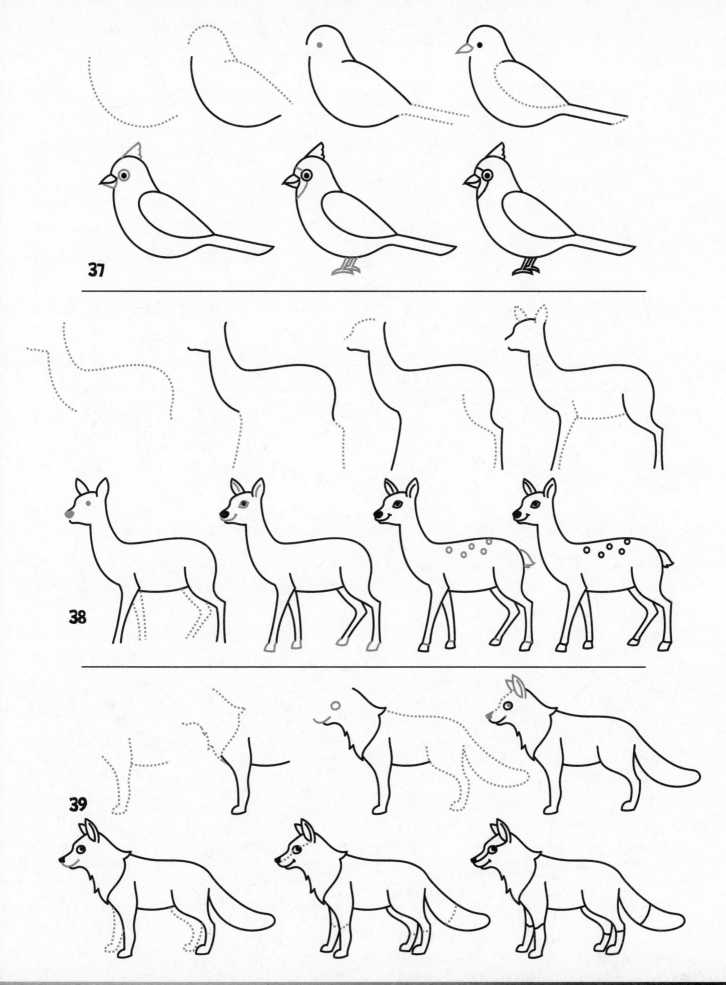

37

38

39

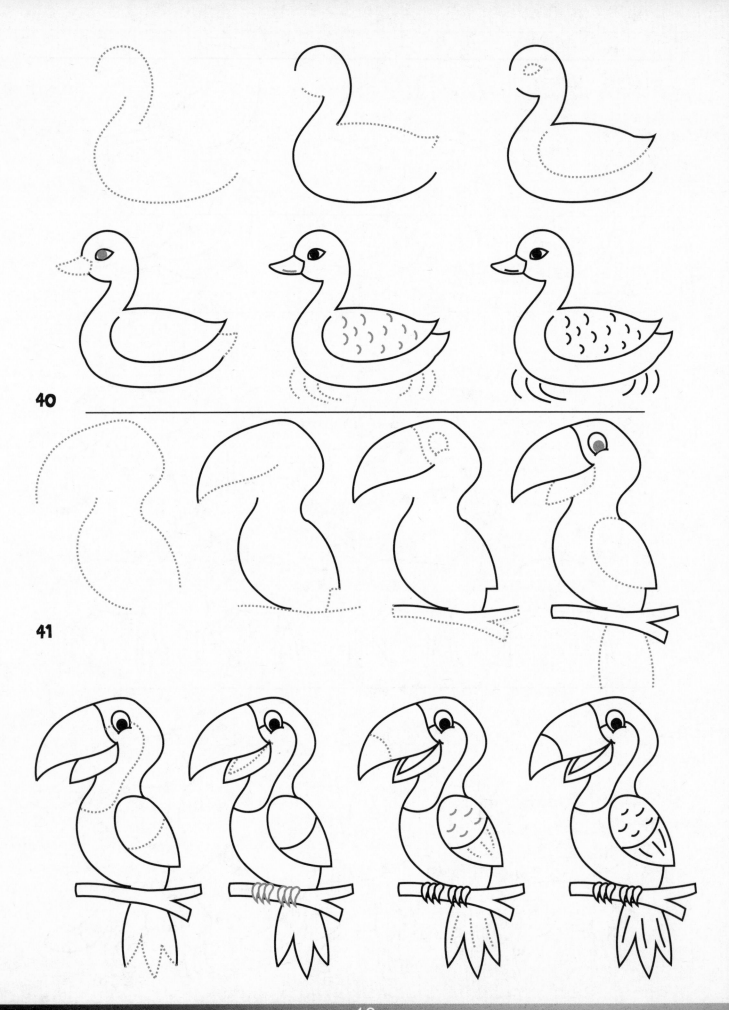

40

41

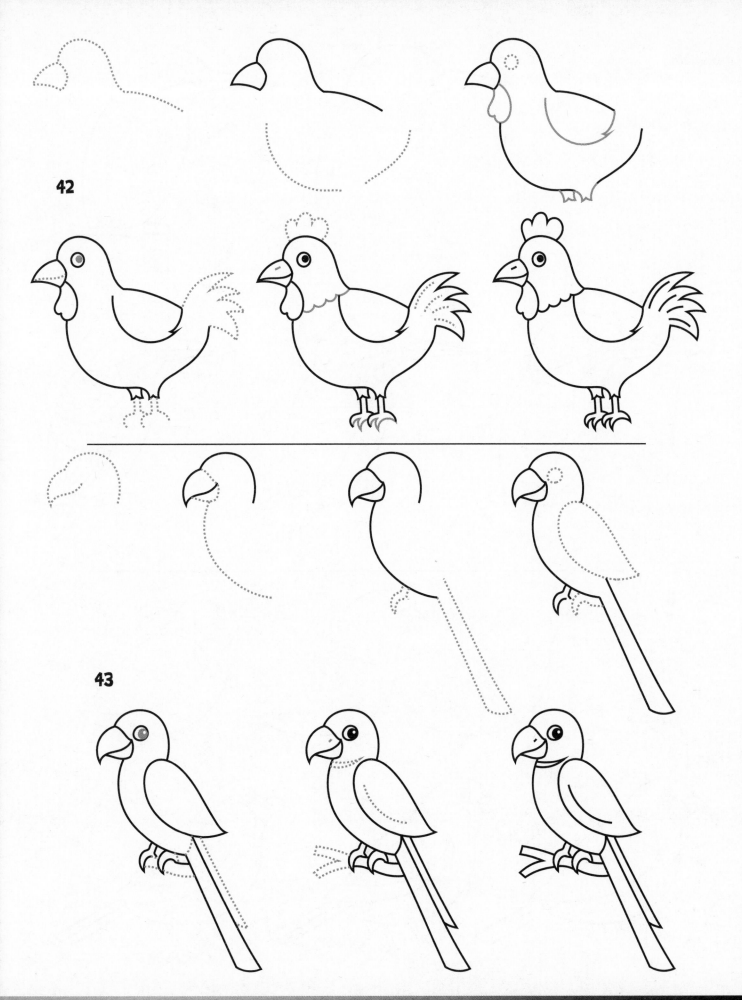

42

43

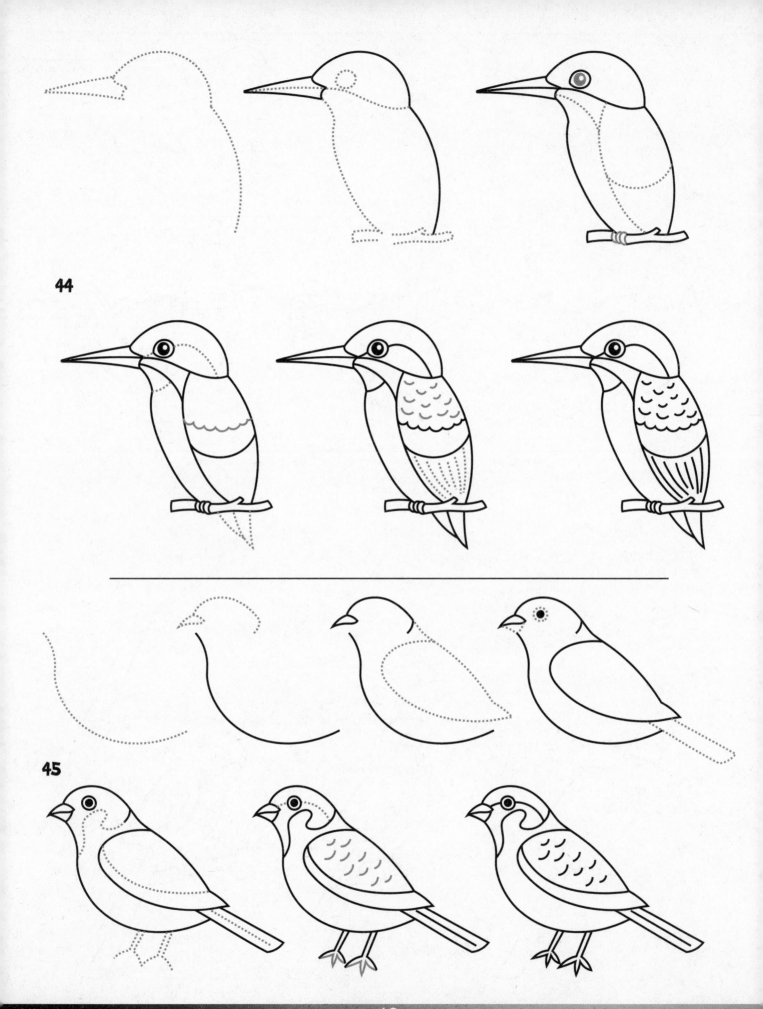

44

45

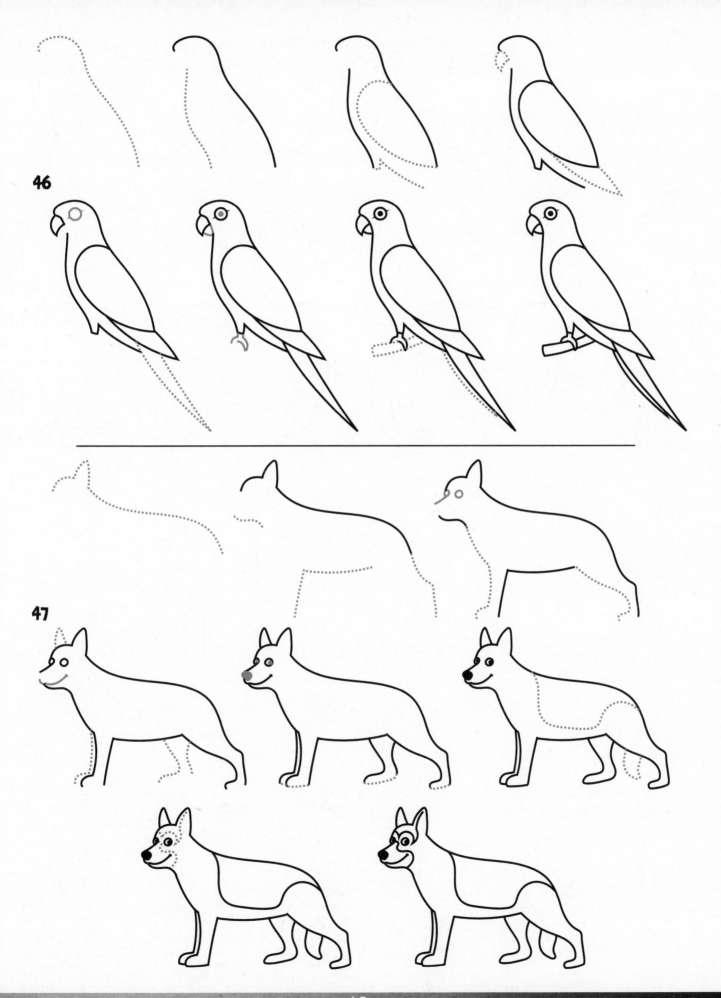

46

47

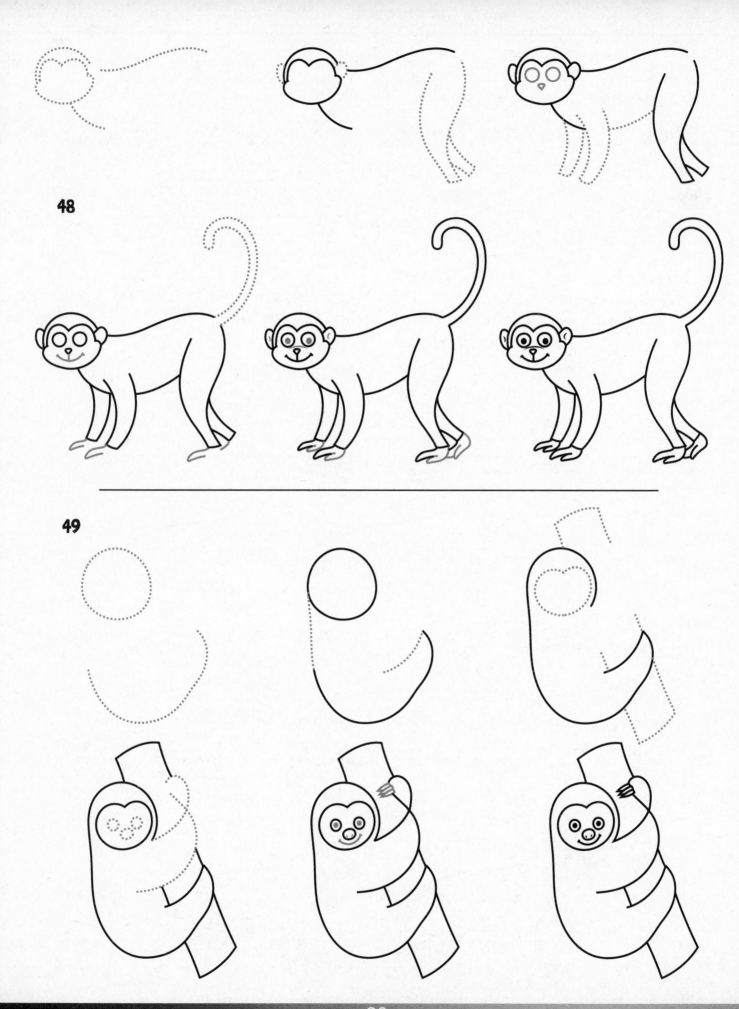

48

49

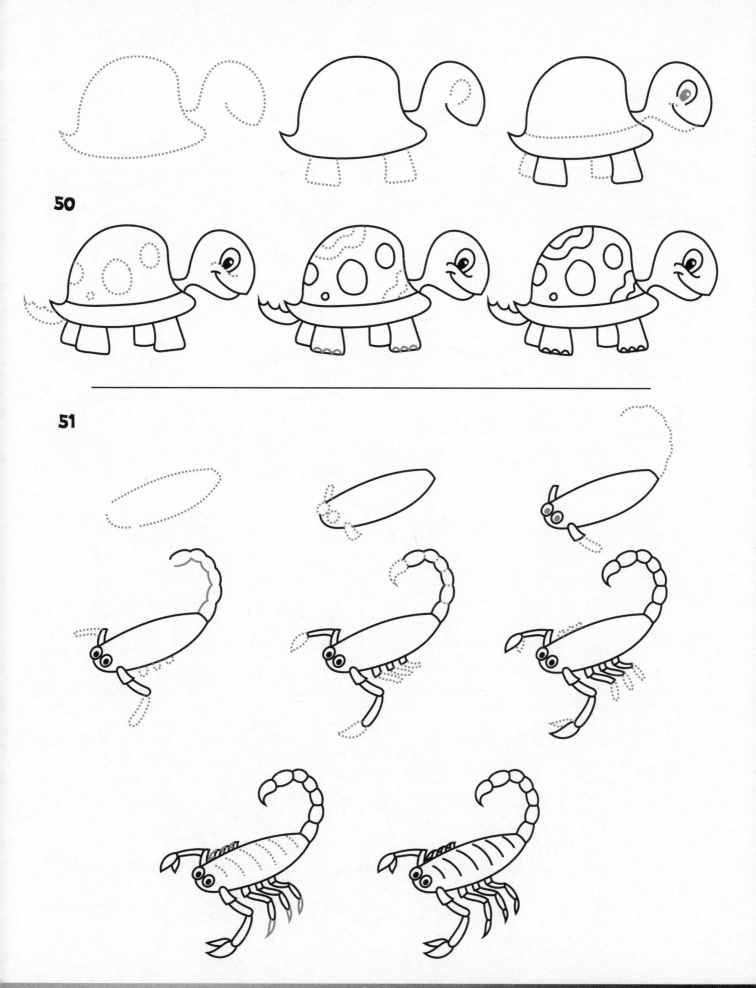

50

51

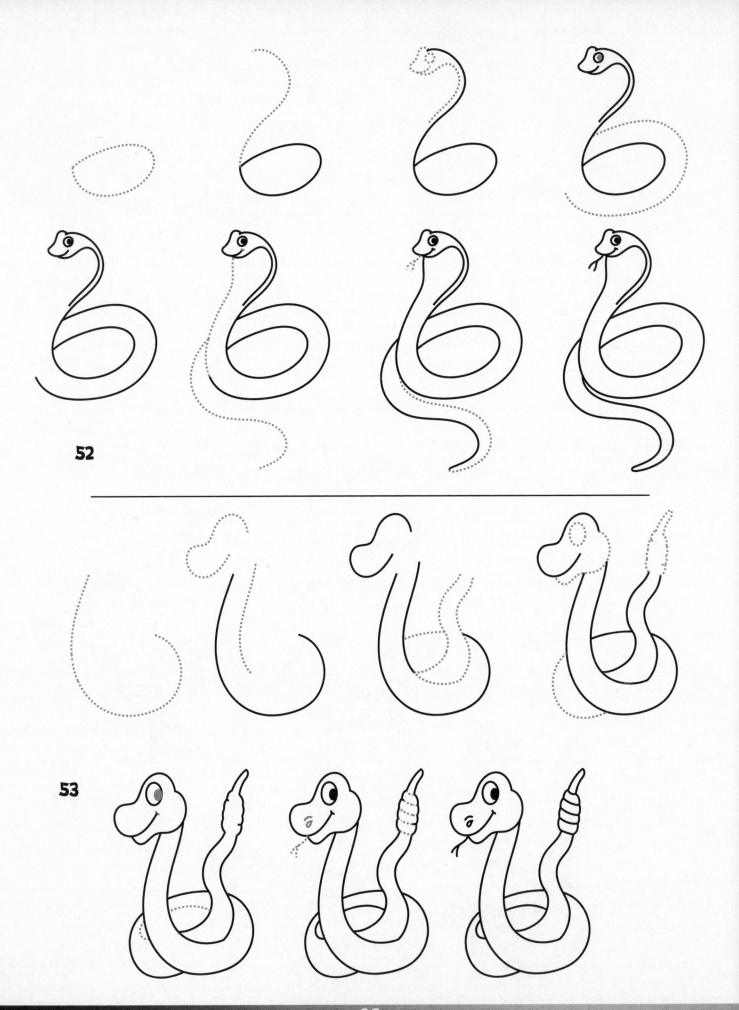

52

53

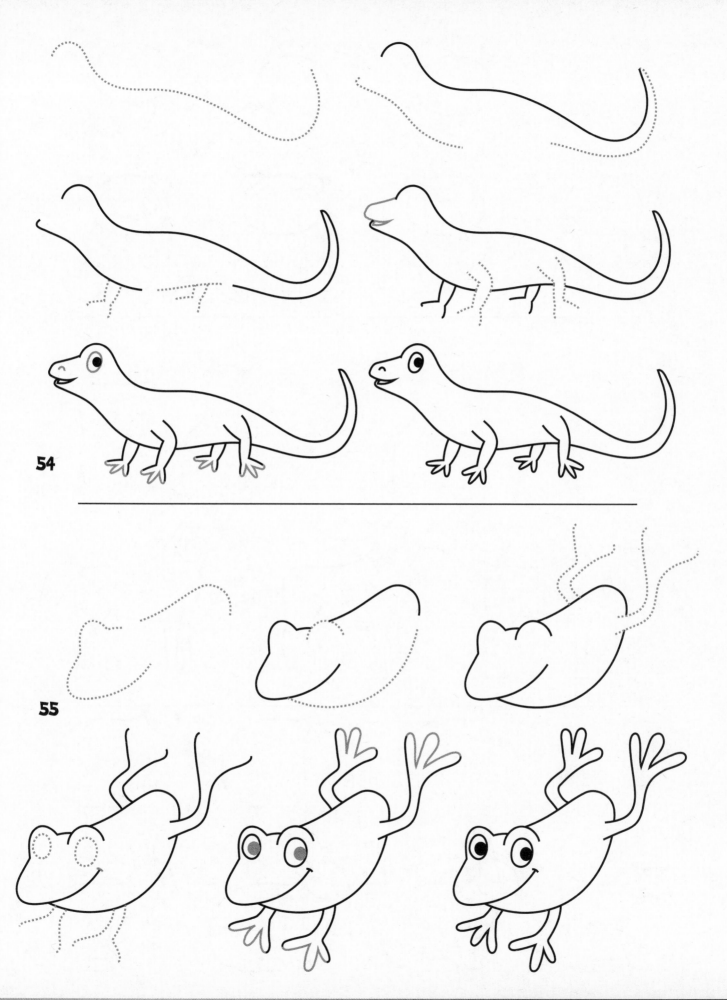

54

55

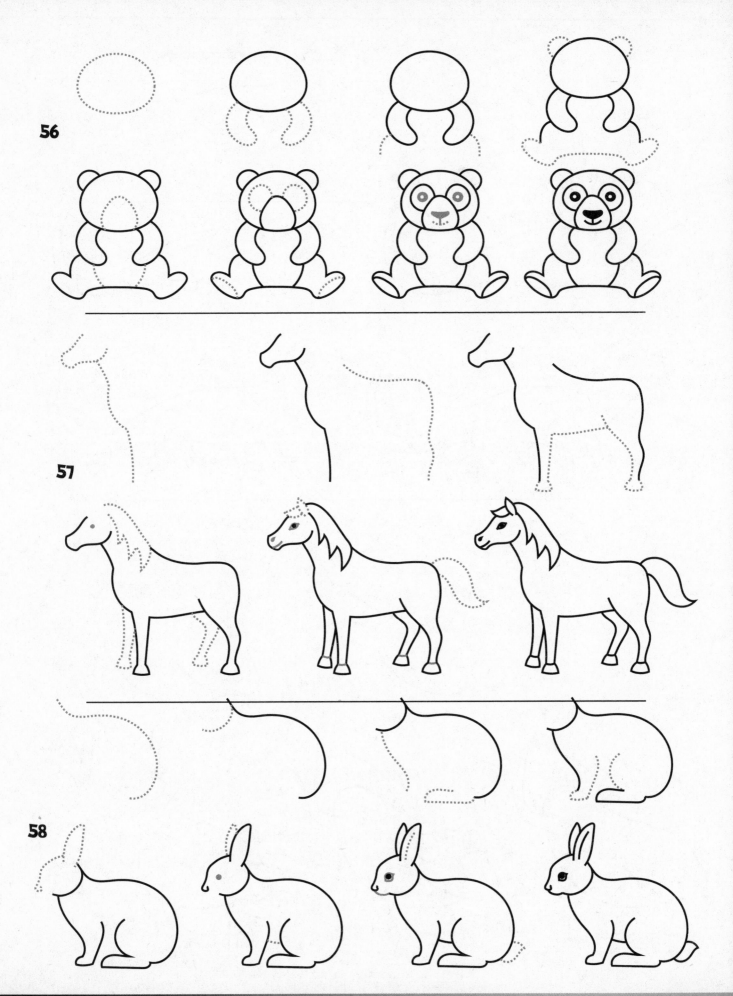

56

57

58

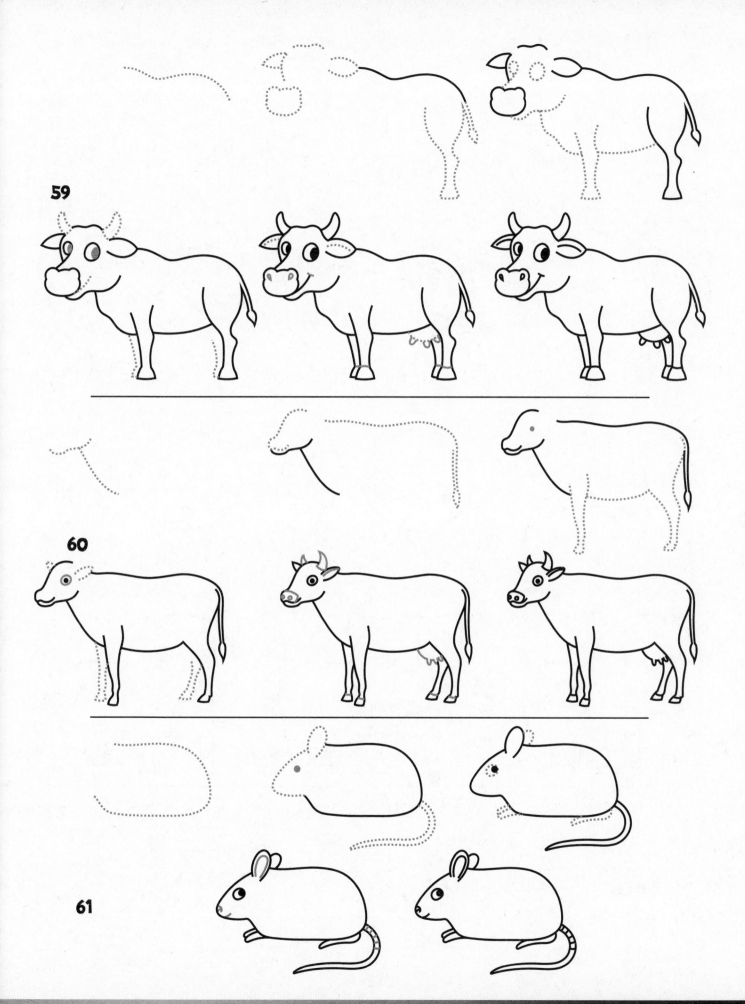

59

60

61

62

63

64

26

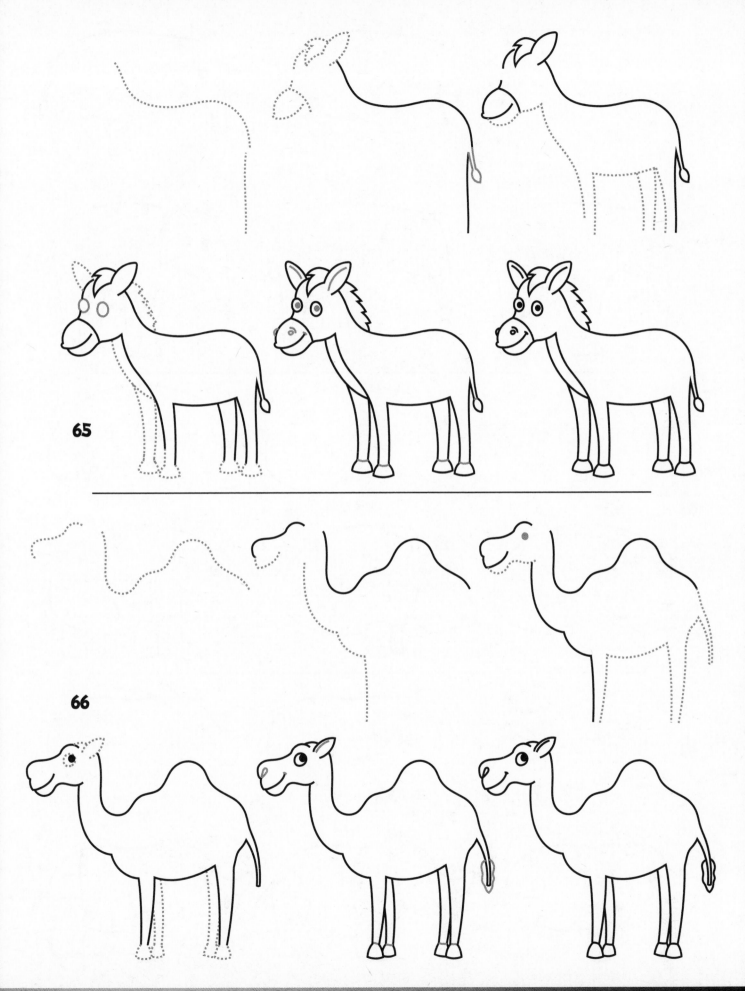

65

66

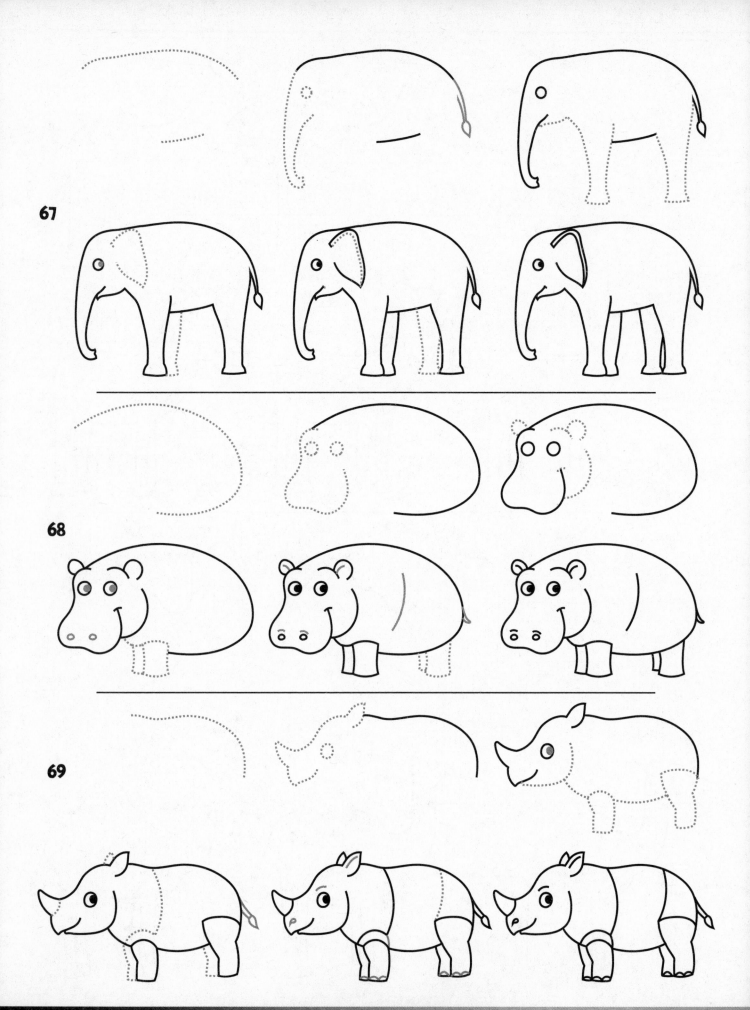

67

68

69

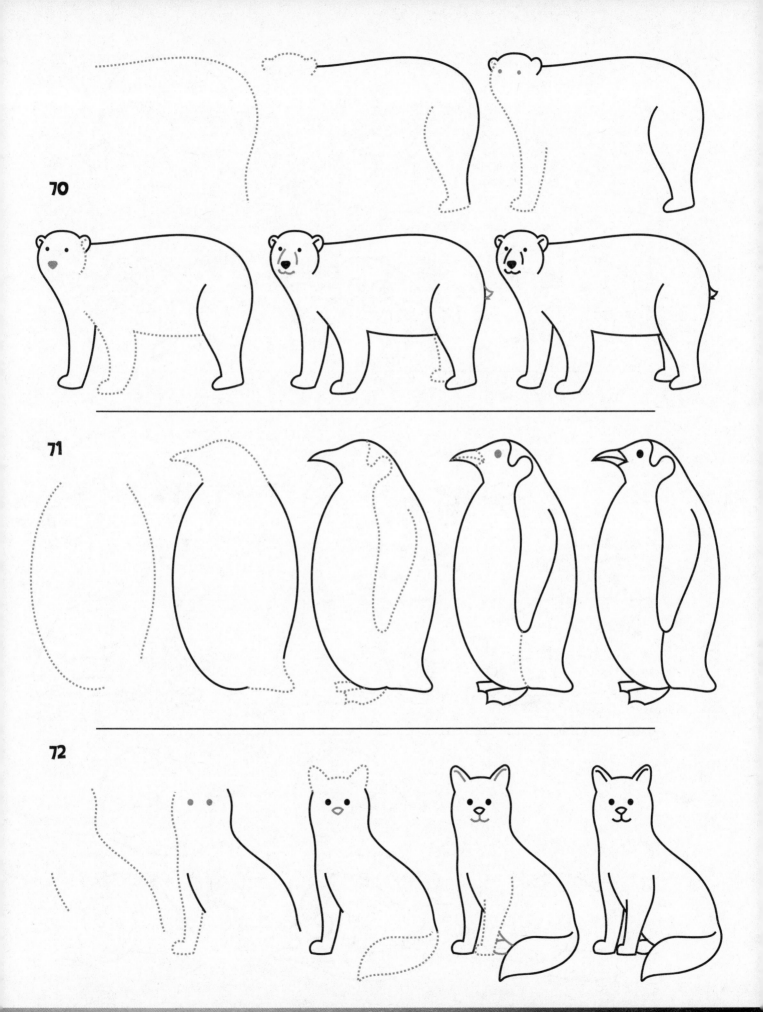

70

71

72

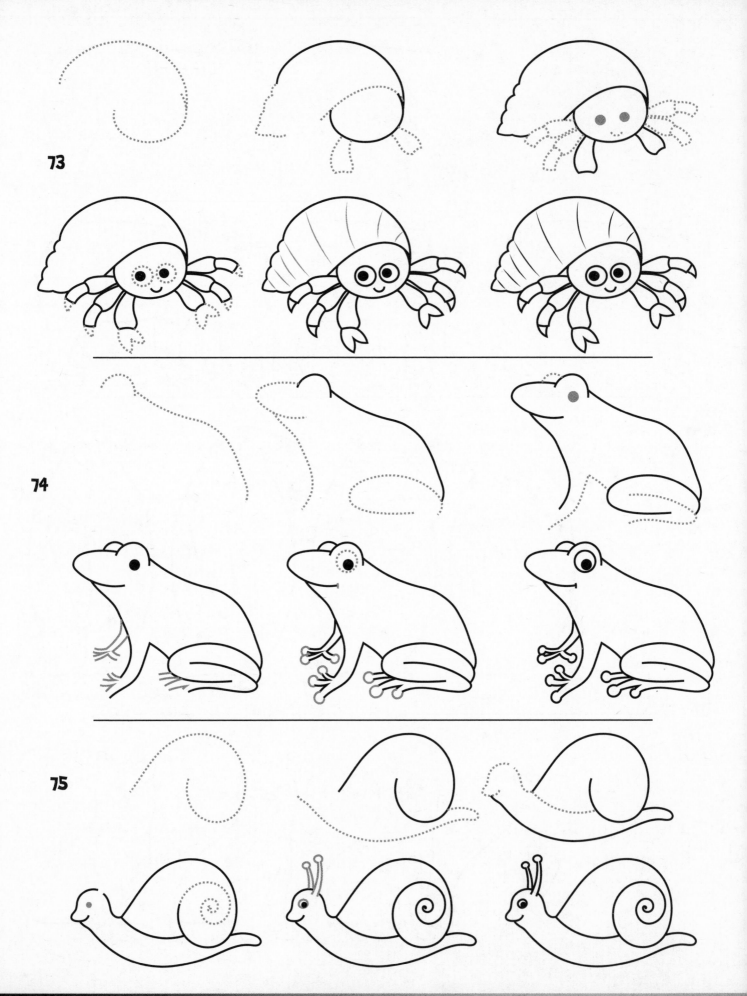

73

74

75

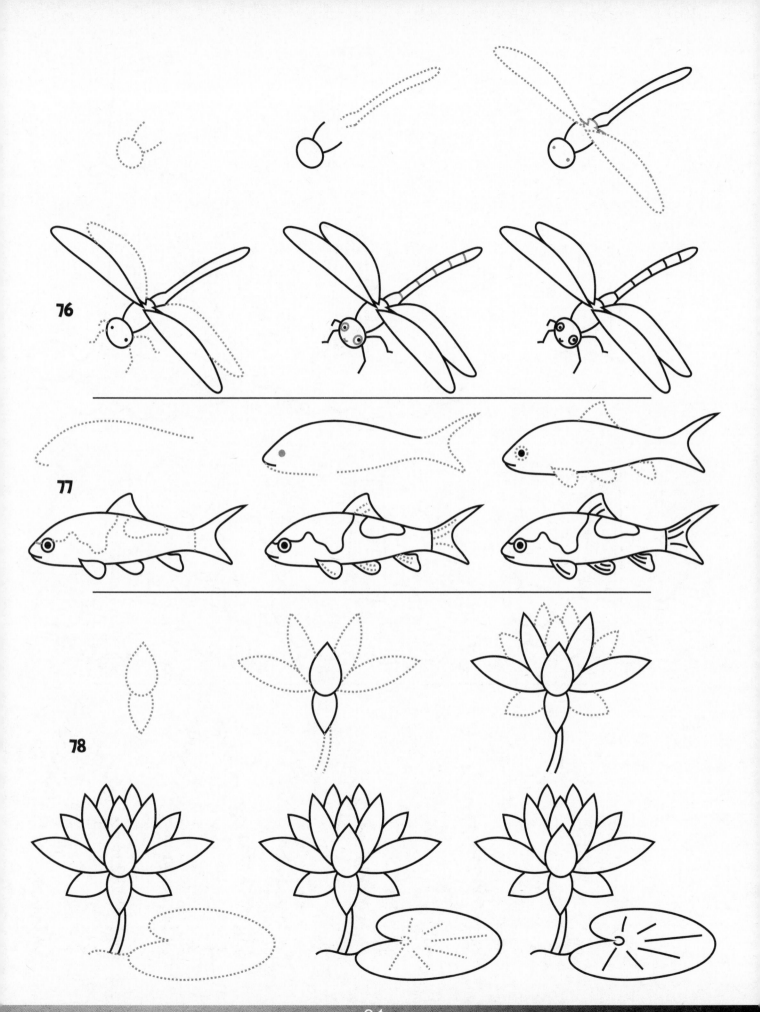

76

77

78

79

80

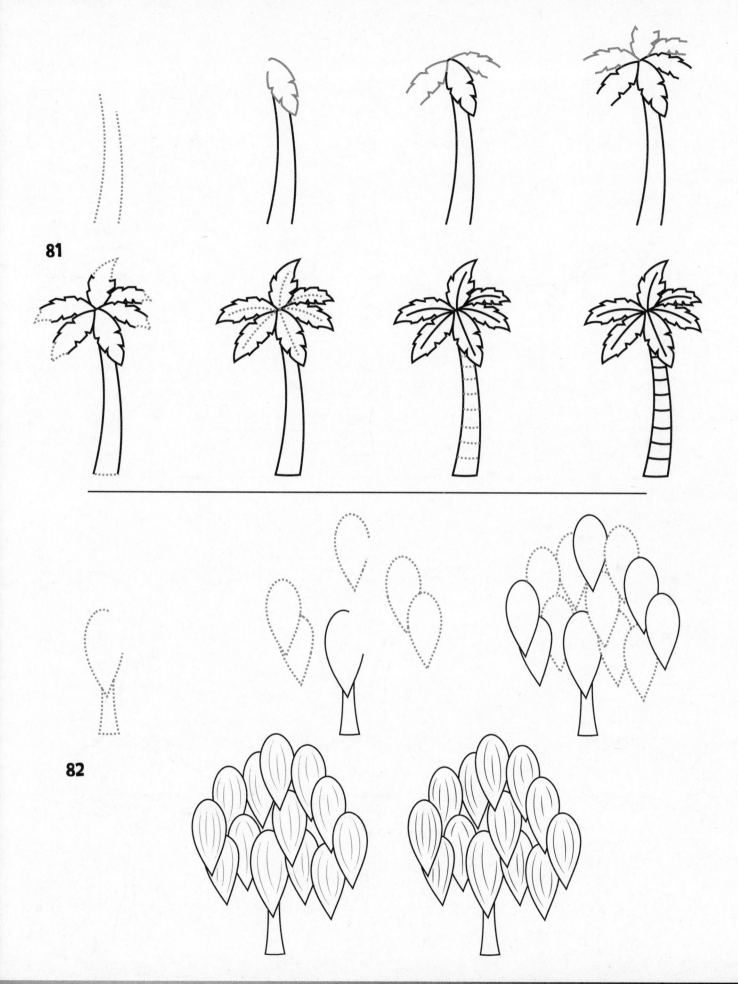

81

82

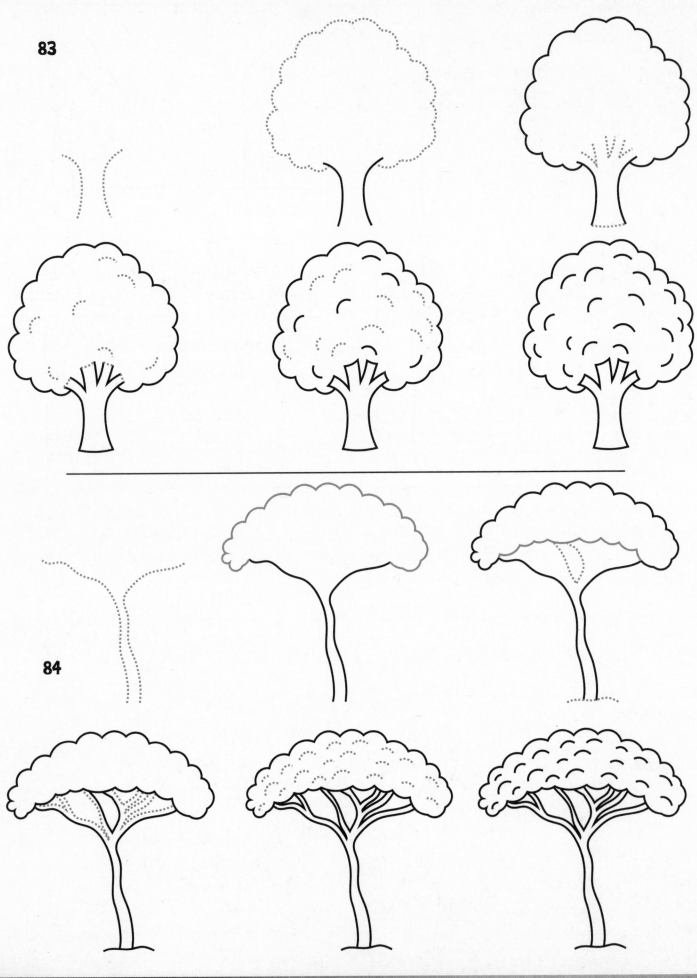

83

84

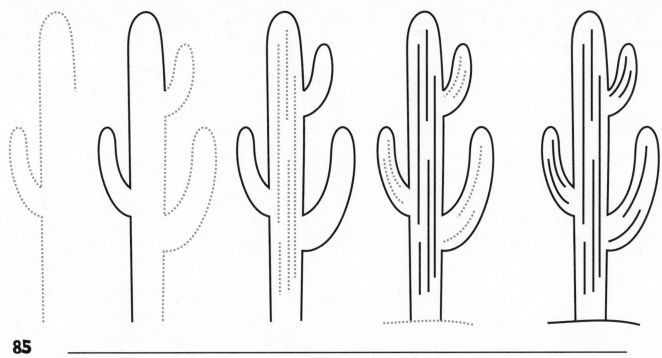

85

86

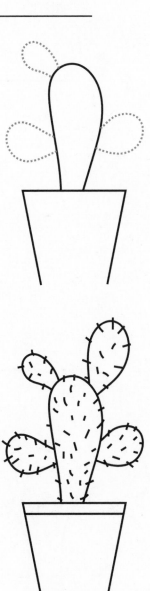

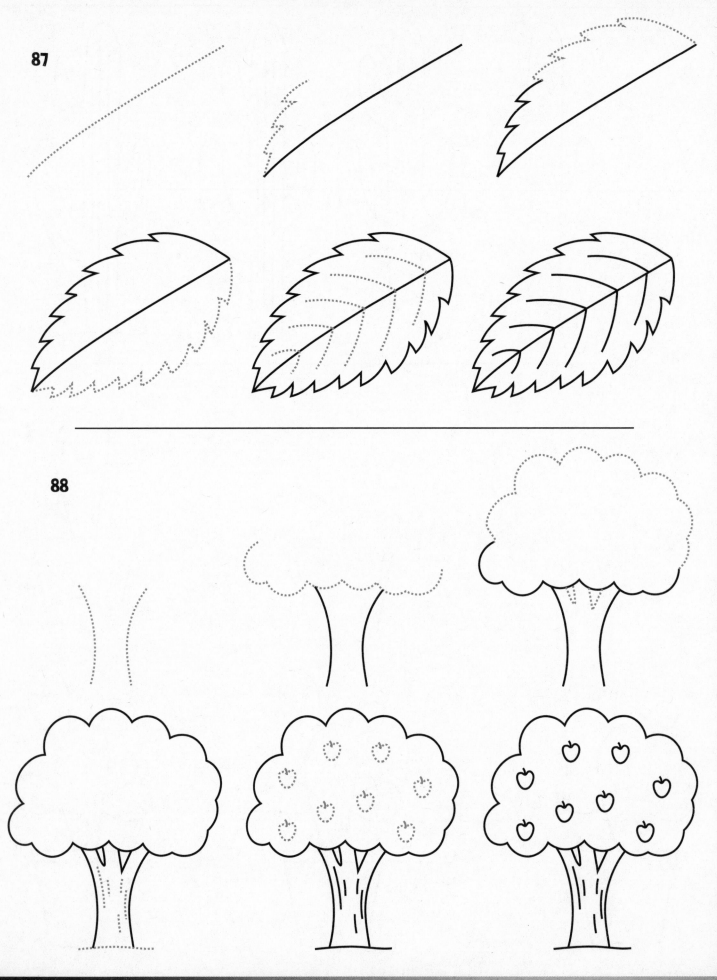

87

88

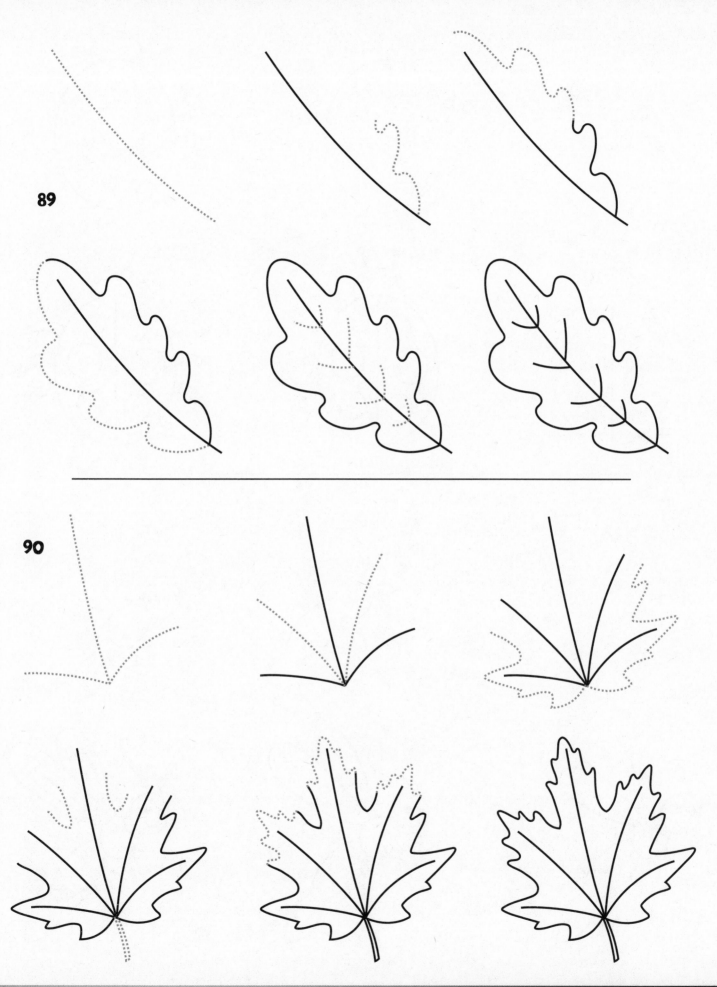

89

90

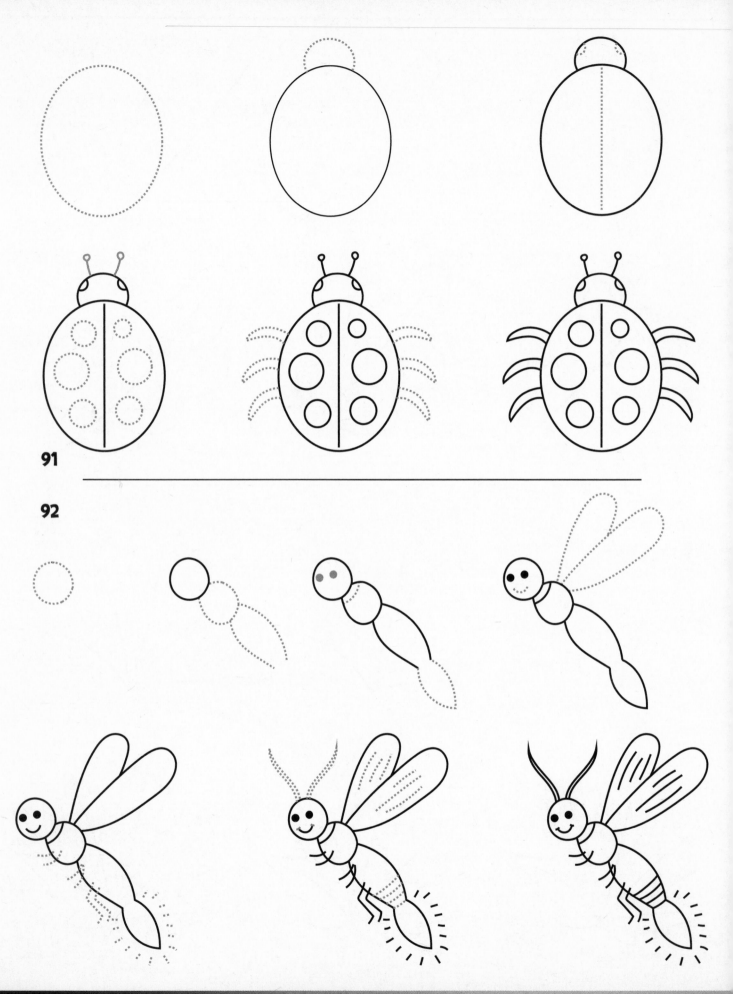

91

92

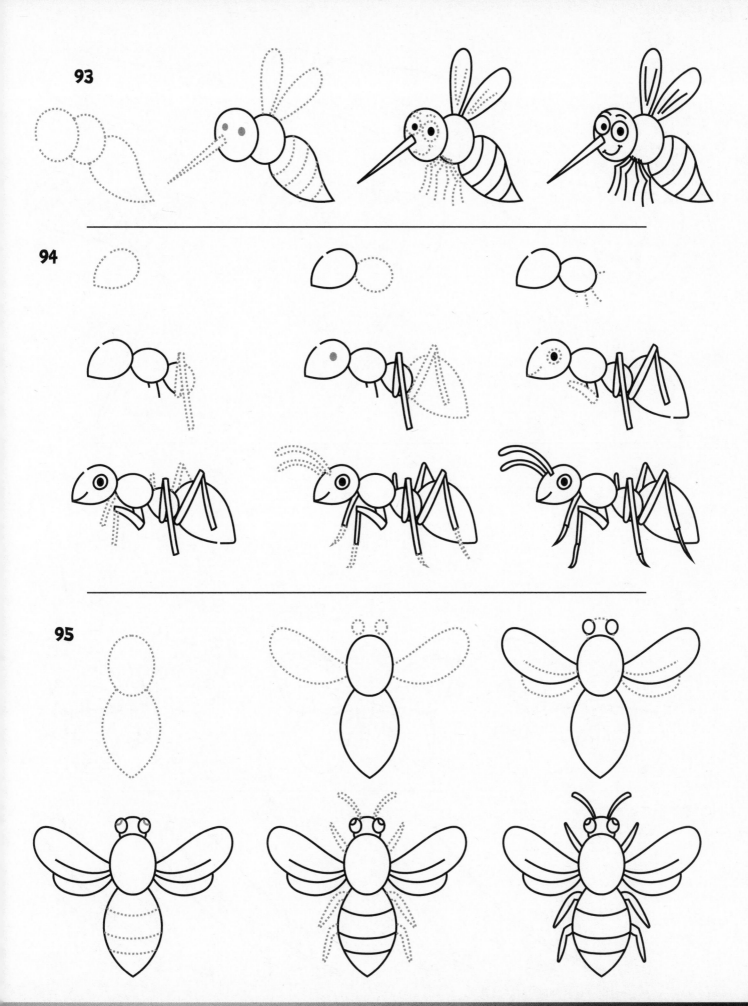

93

94

95

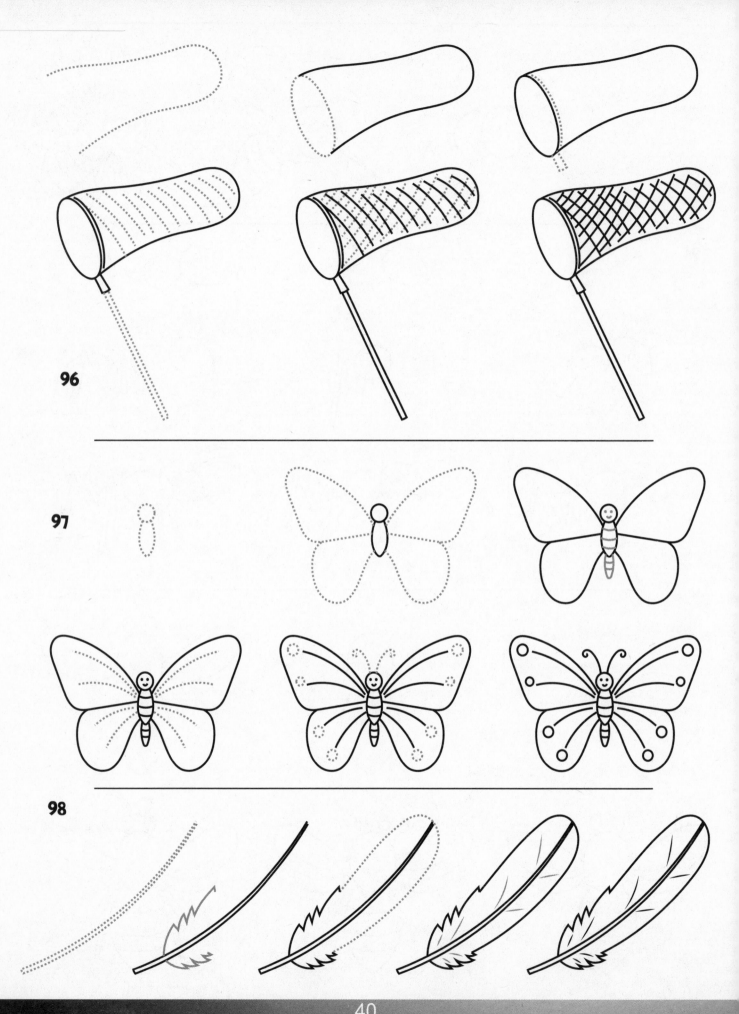

96

97

98

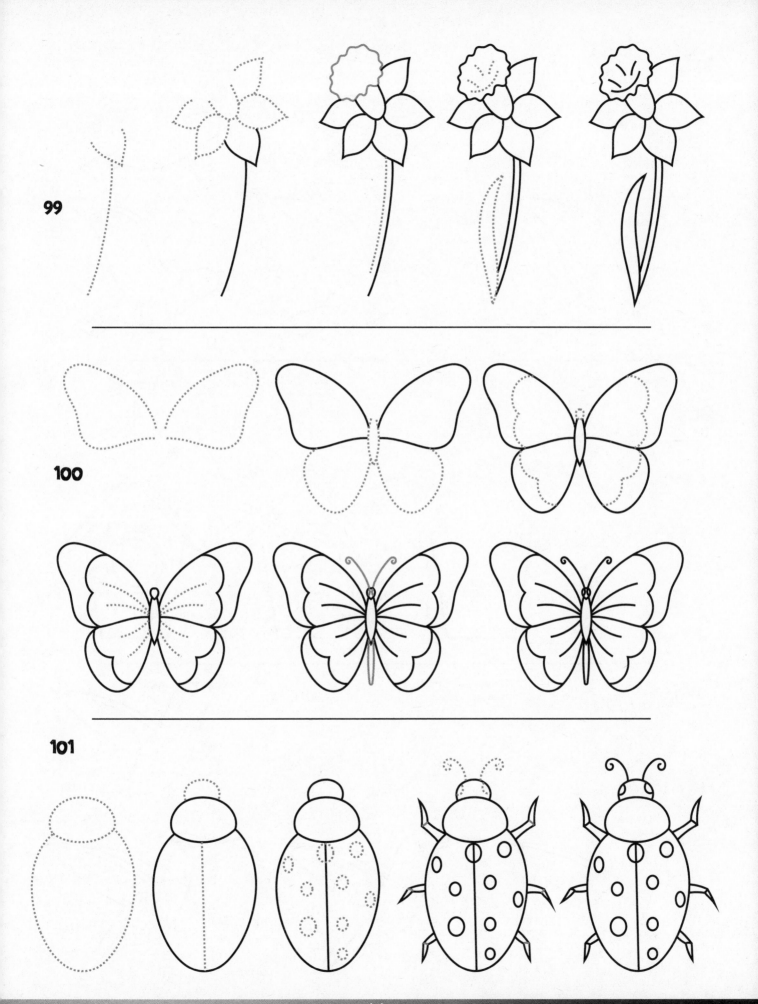

99

100

101

102

103

104

105

106

107

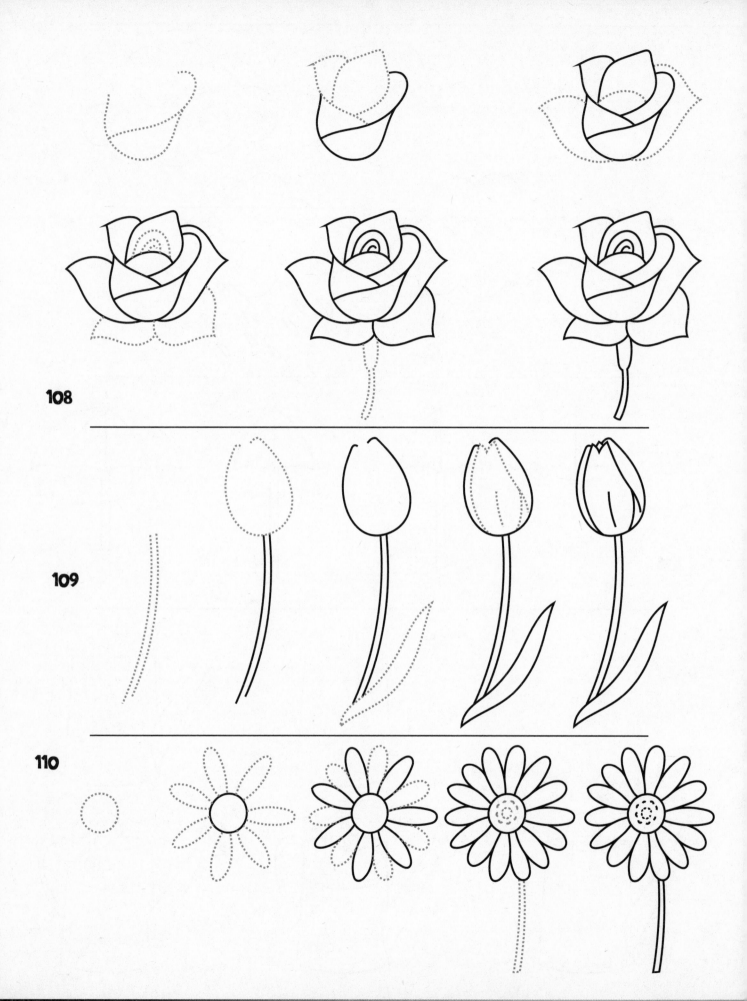

108

109

110

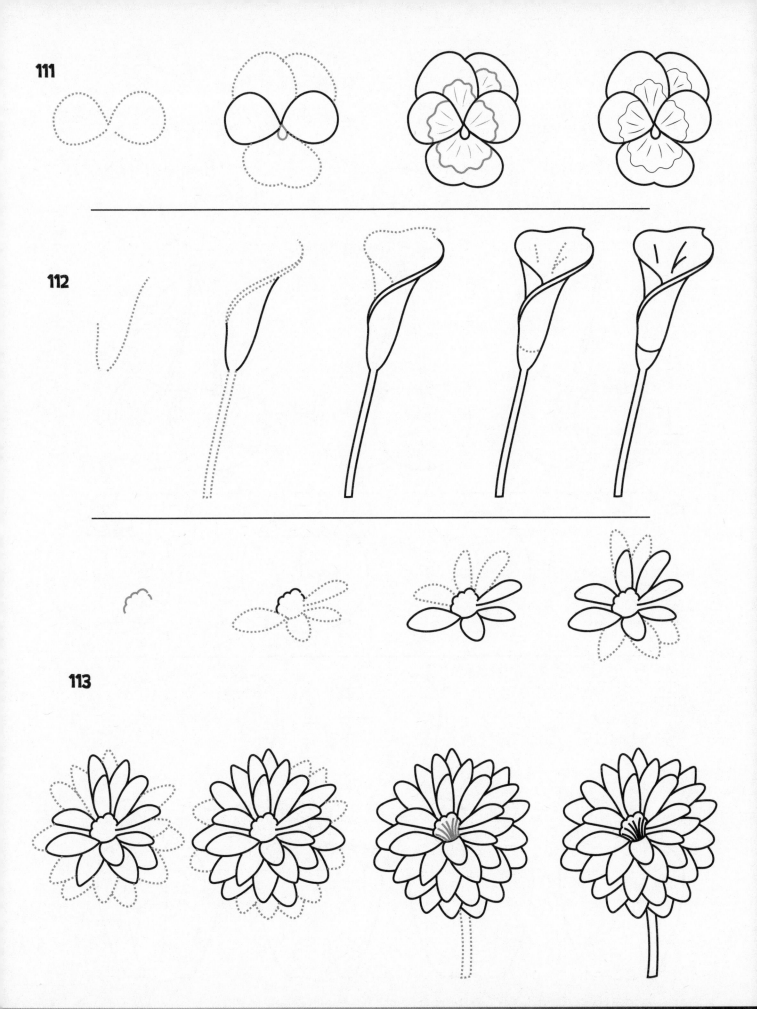

111

112

113

114

115

116

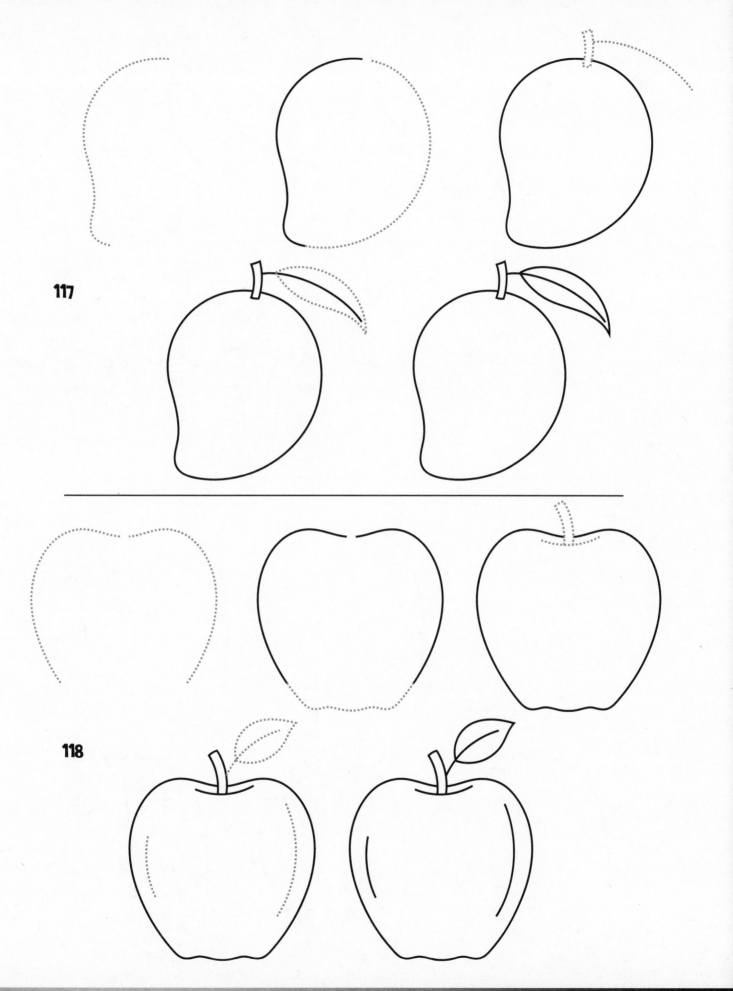

117

118

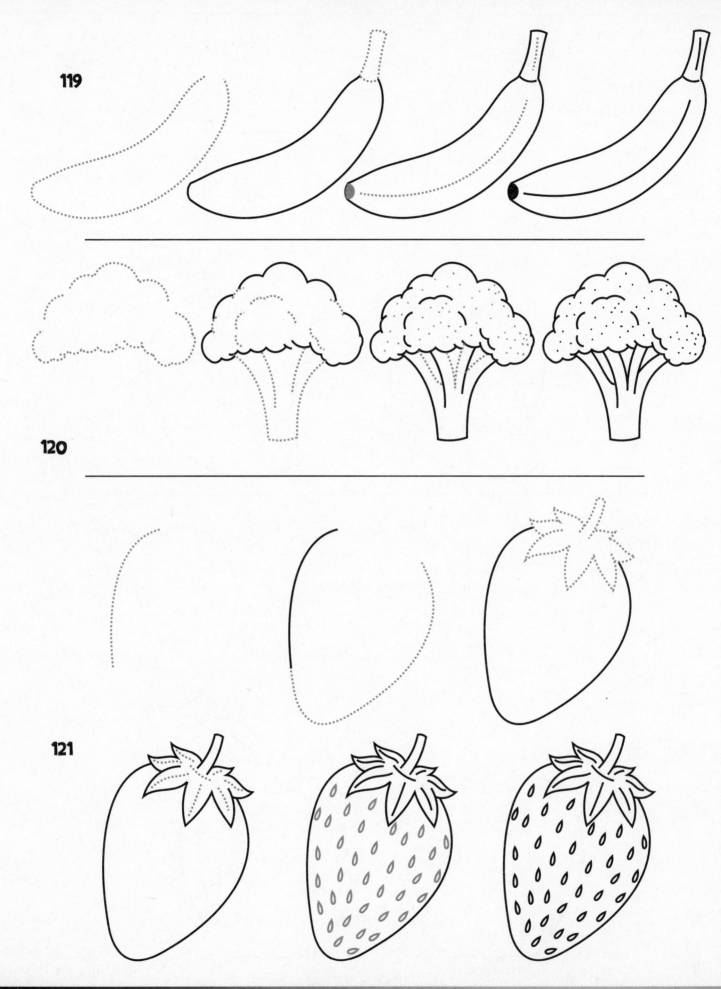

119

120

121

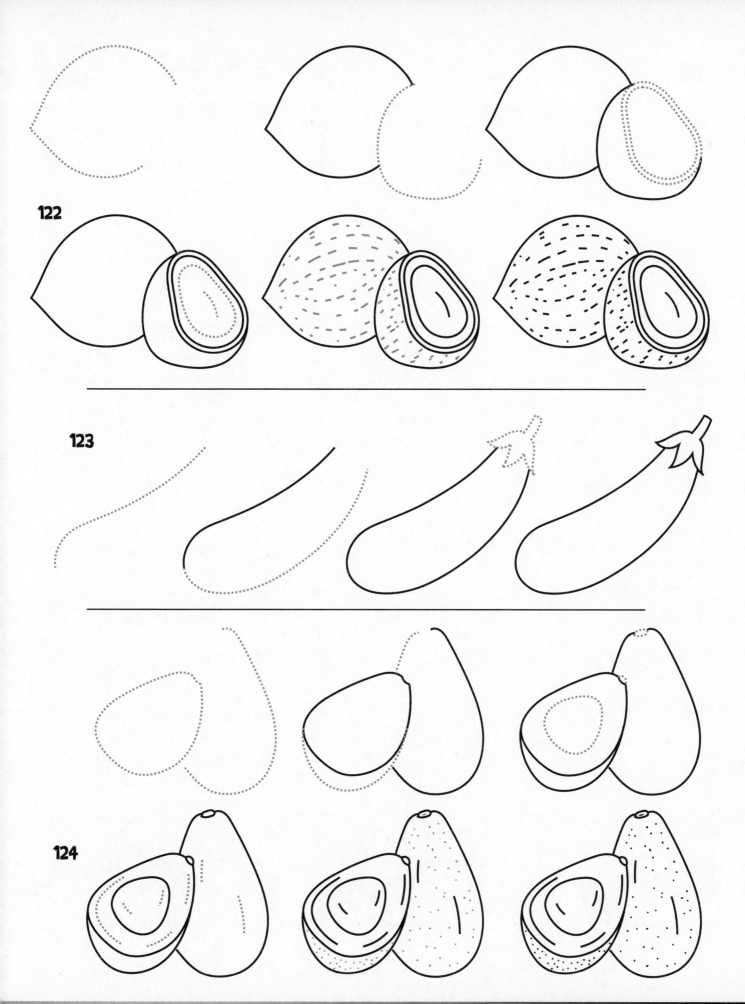

122

123

124

125

126

127

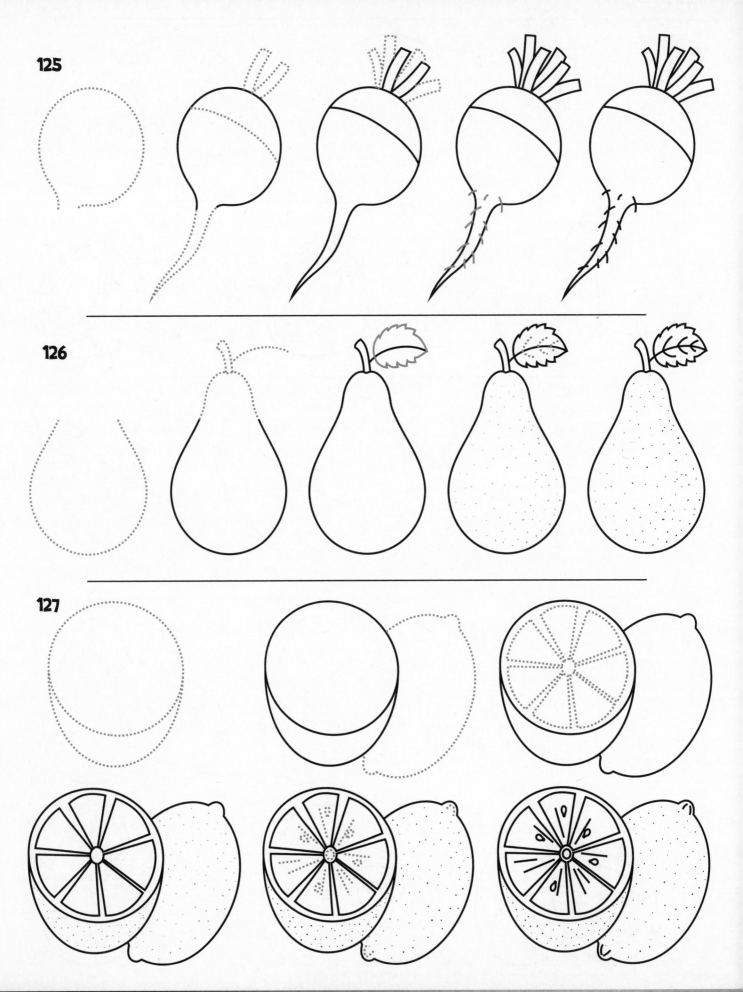

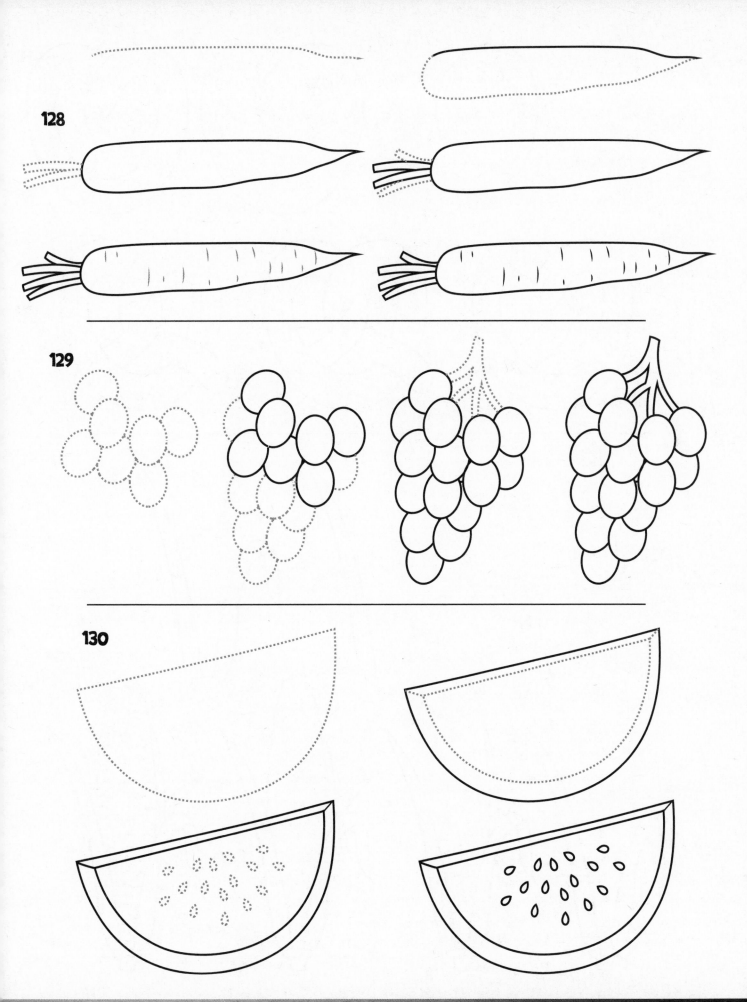

128

129

130

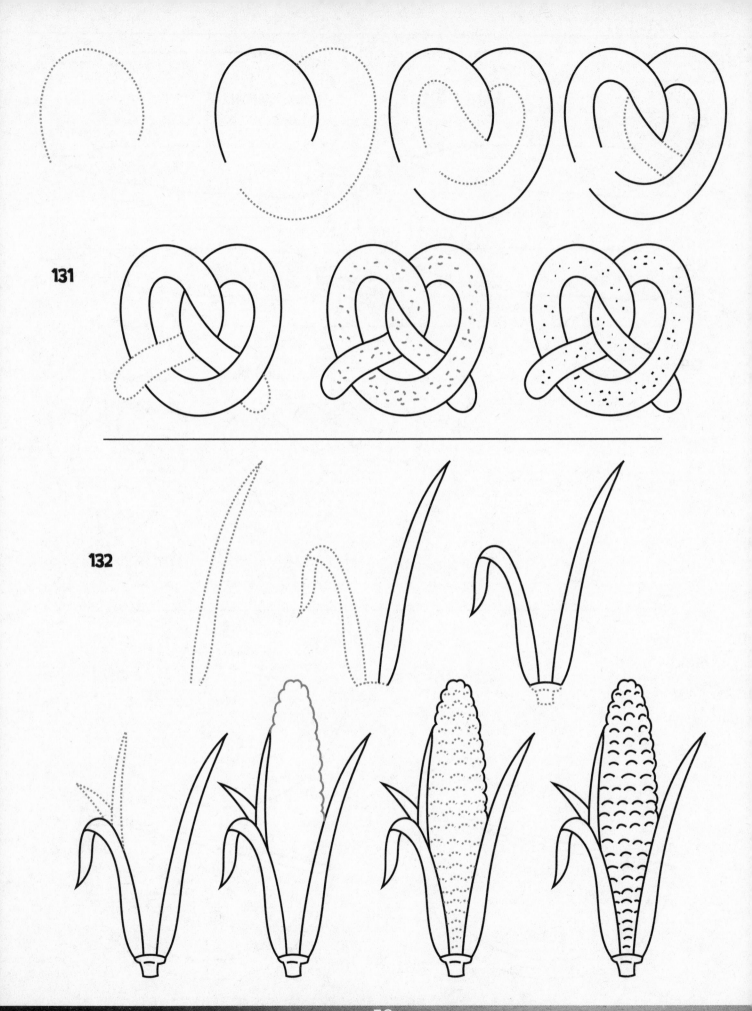

131

132

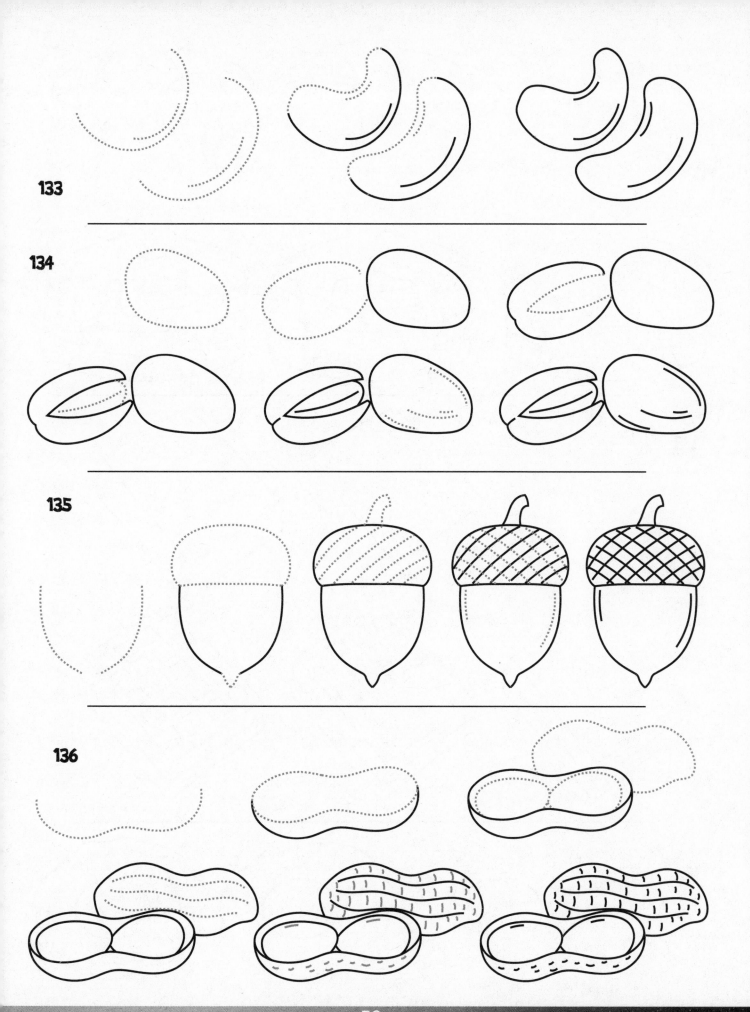

133

134

135

136

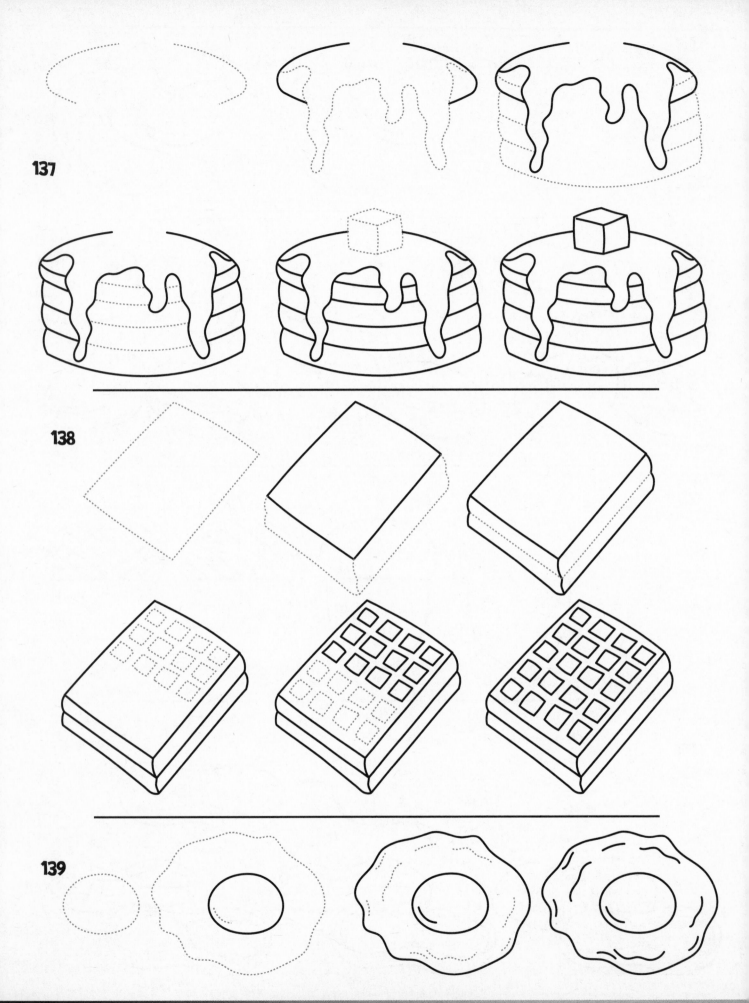

137

138

139

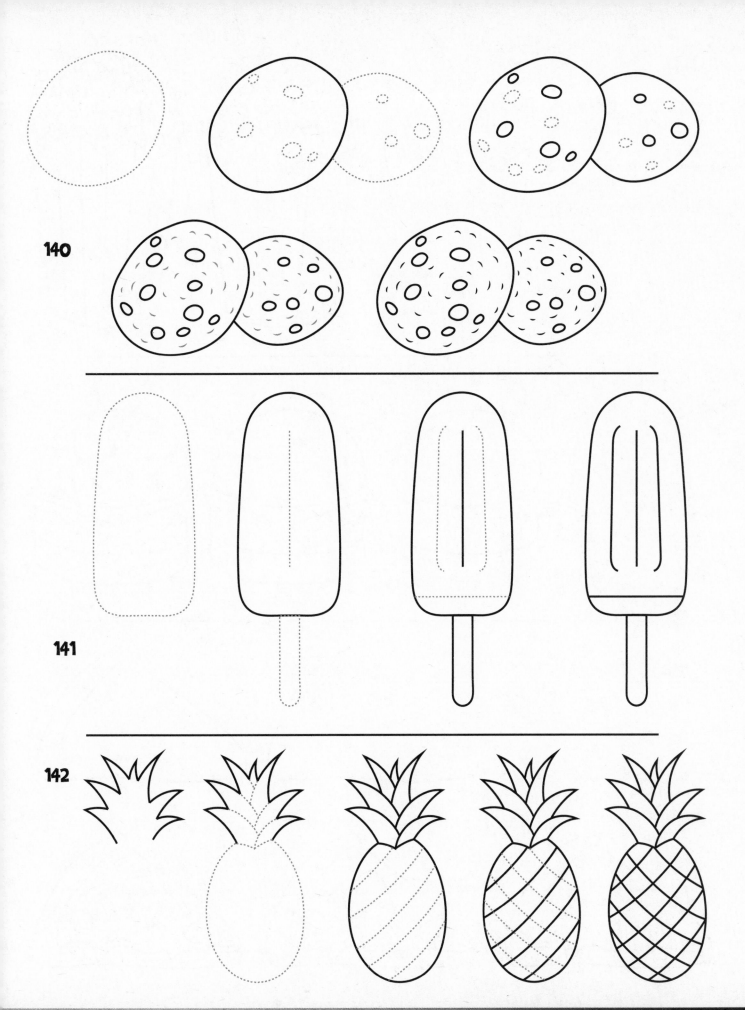

140

141

142

143

144

145

146

147

148

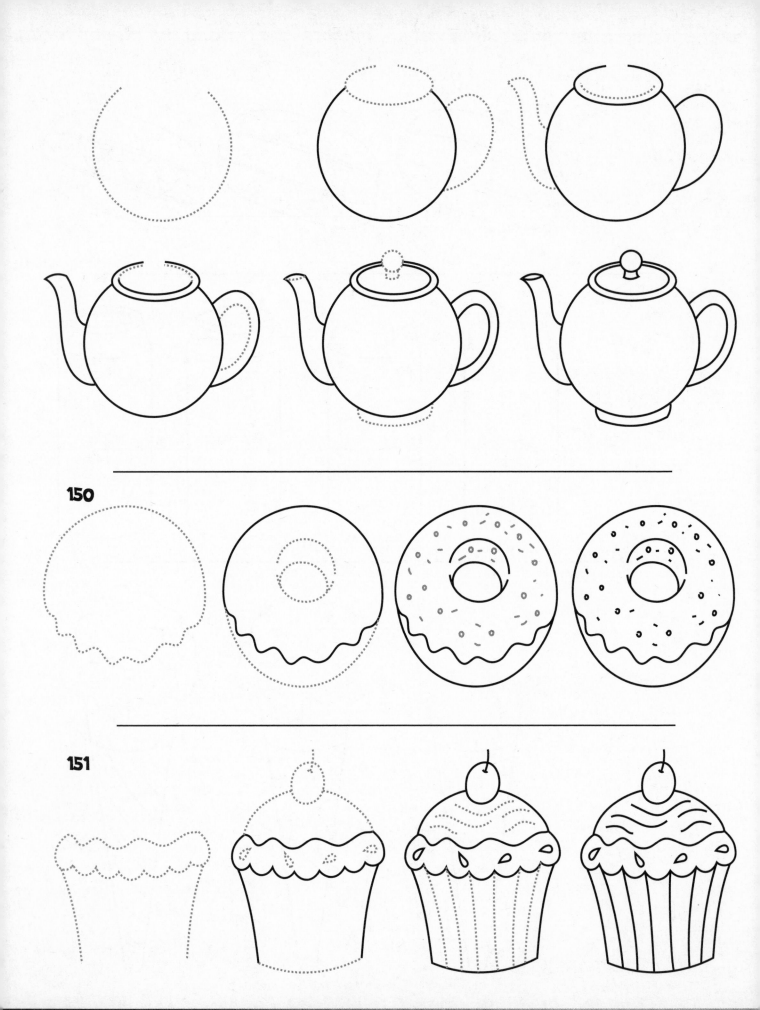

150

151

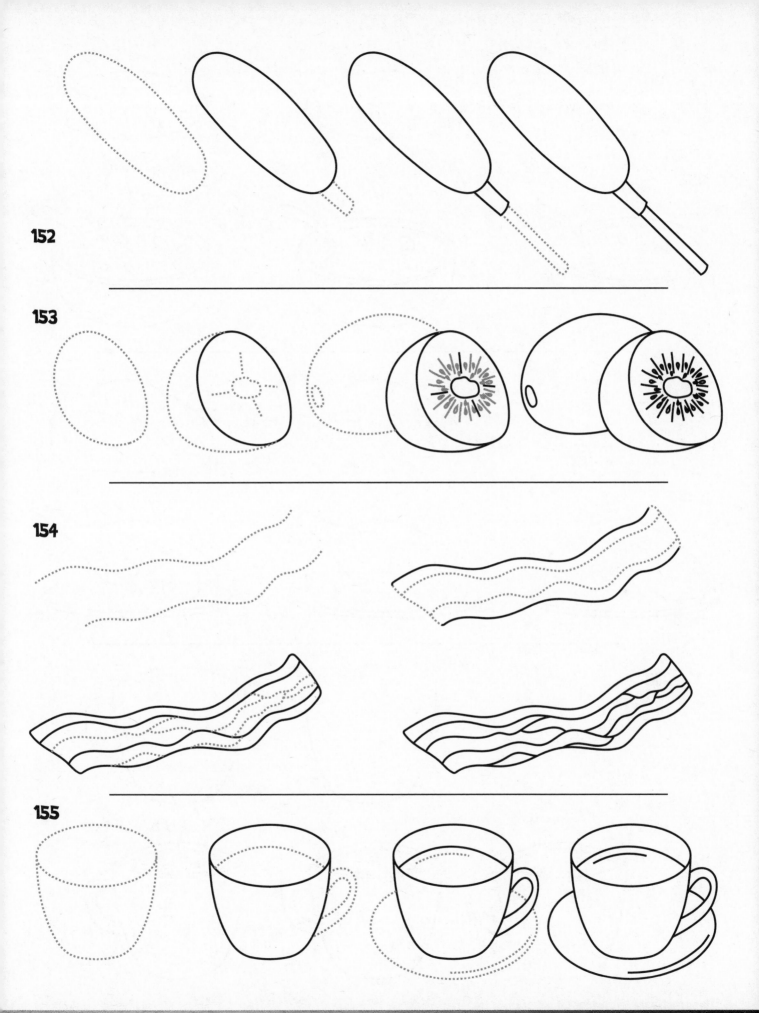

152

153

154

155

156

157

158

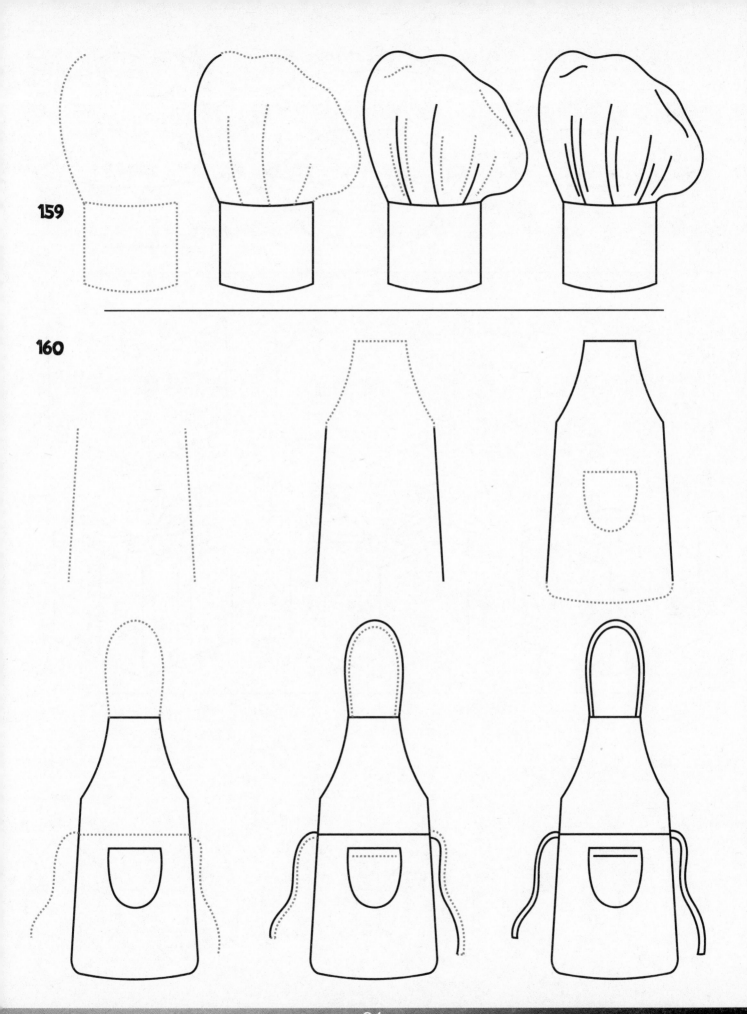

159

160

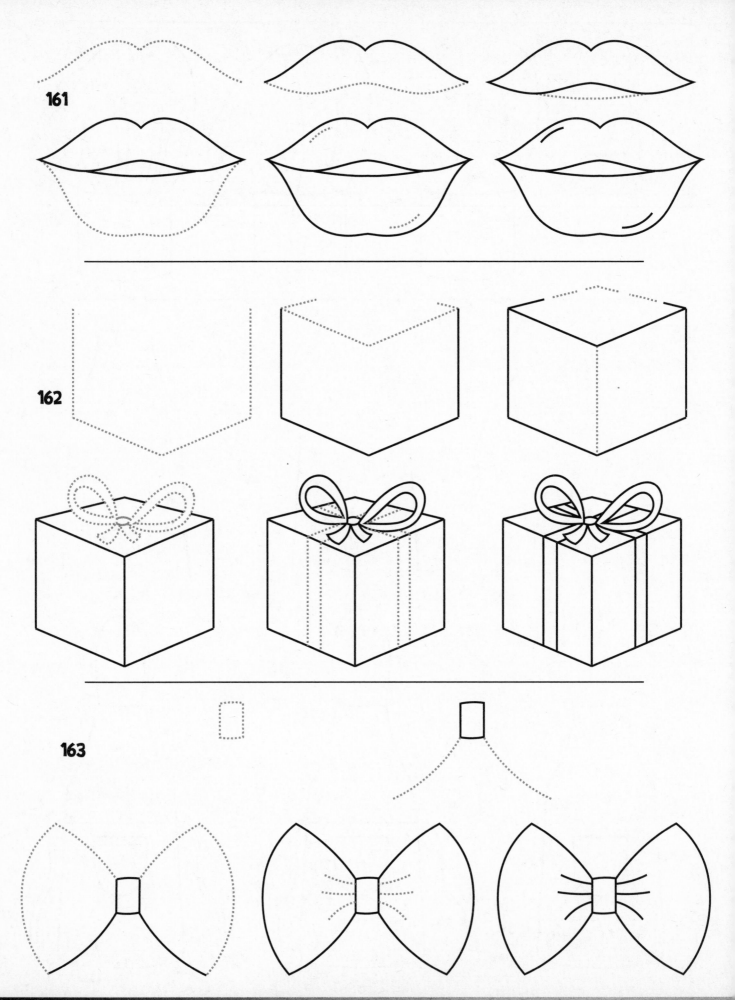

161

162

163

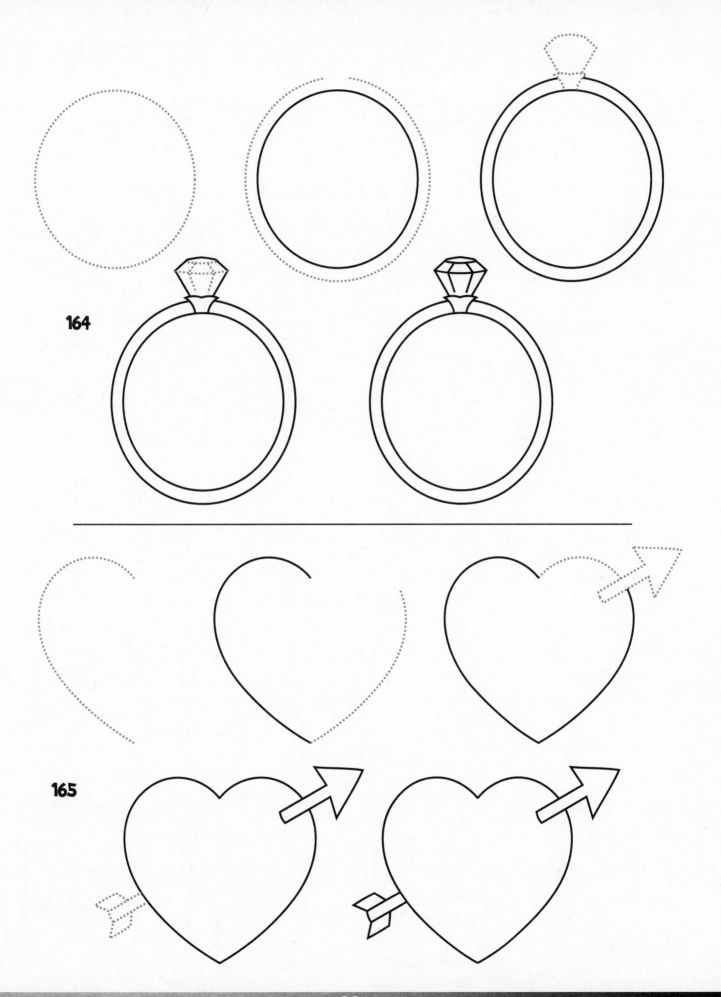

164

165

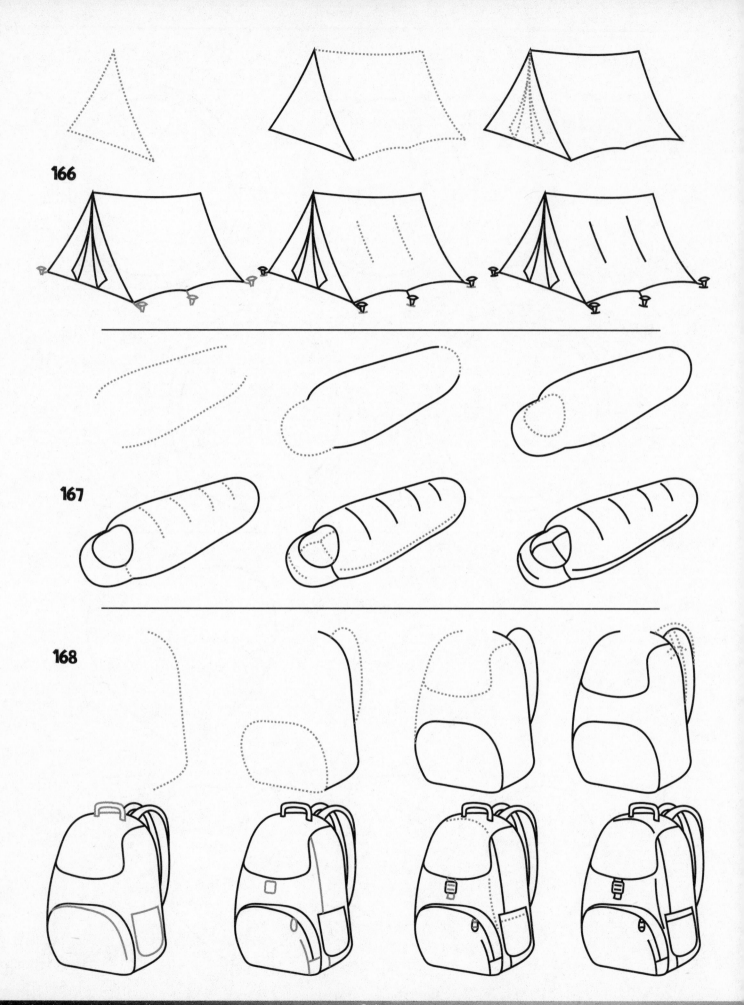

166

167

168

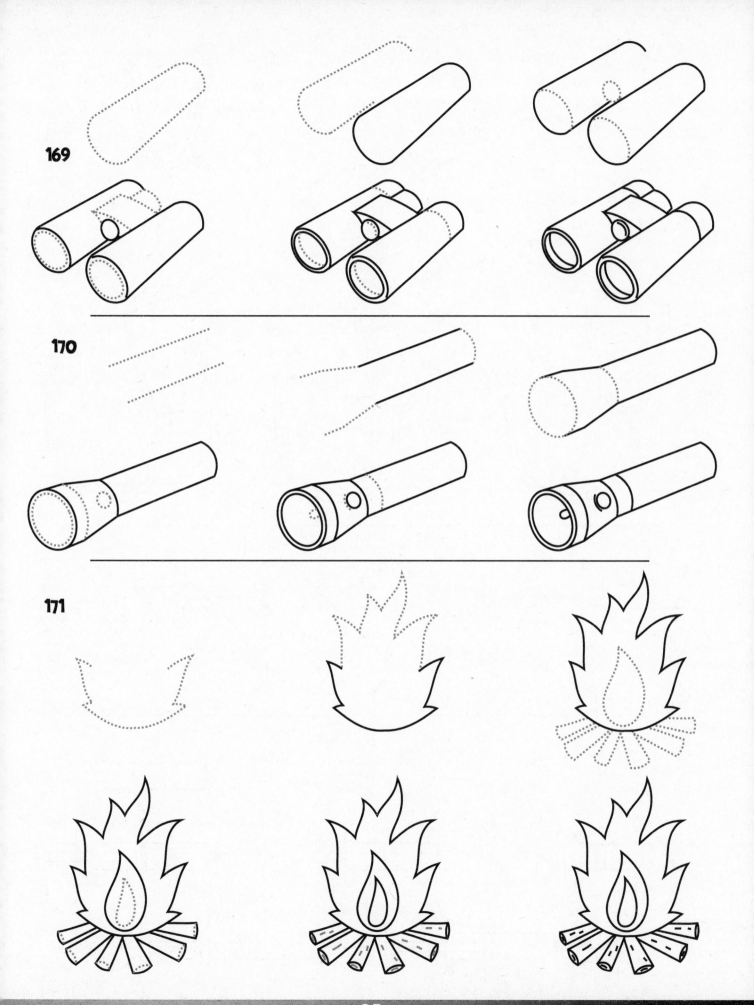

169

170

171

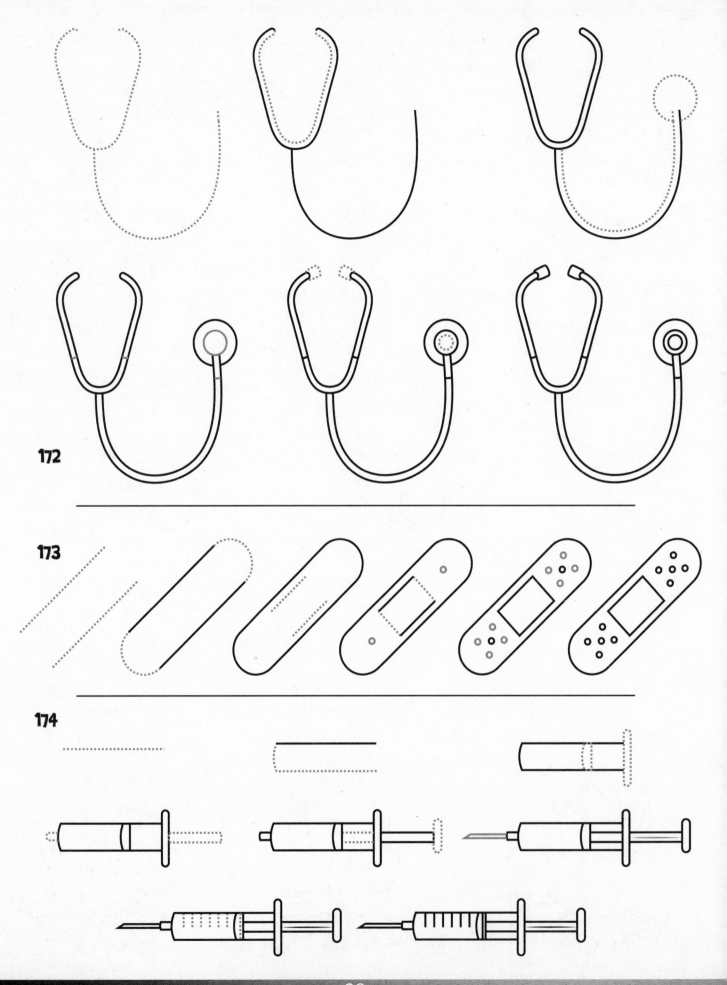

172

173

174

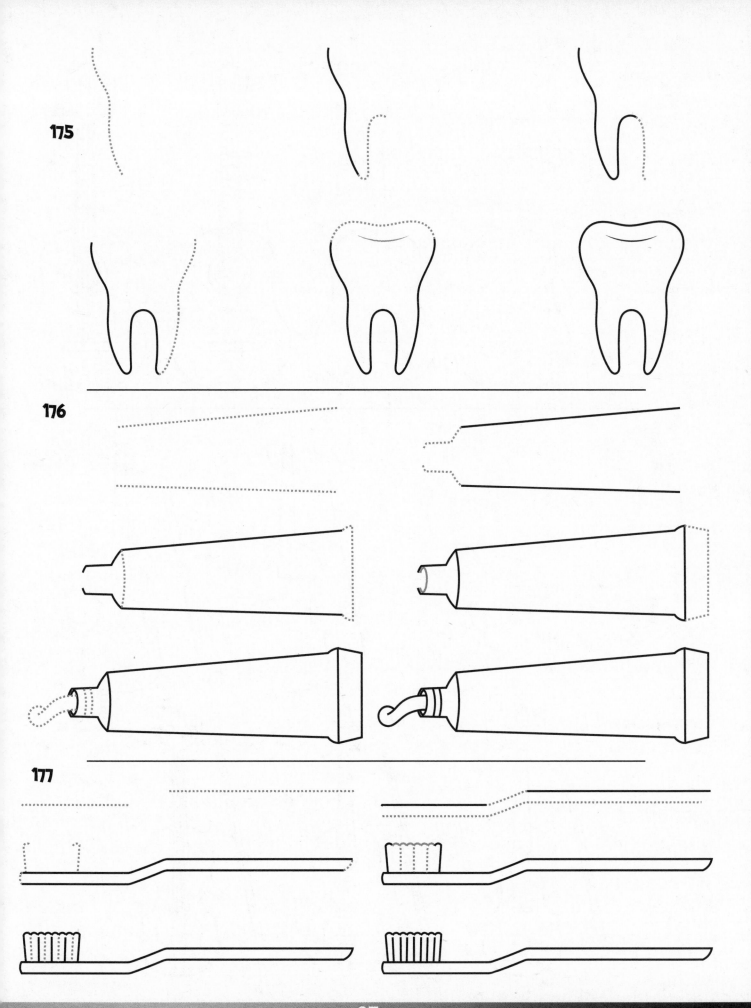

175

176

177

178

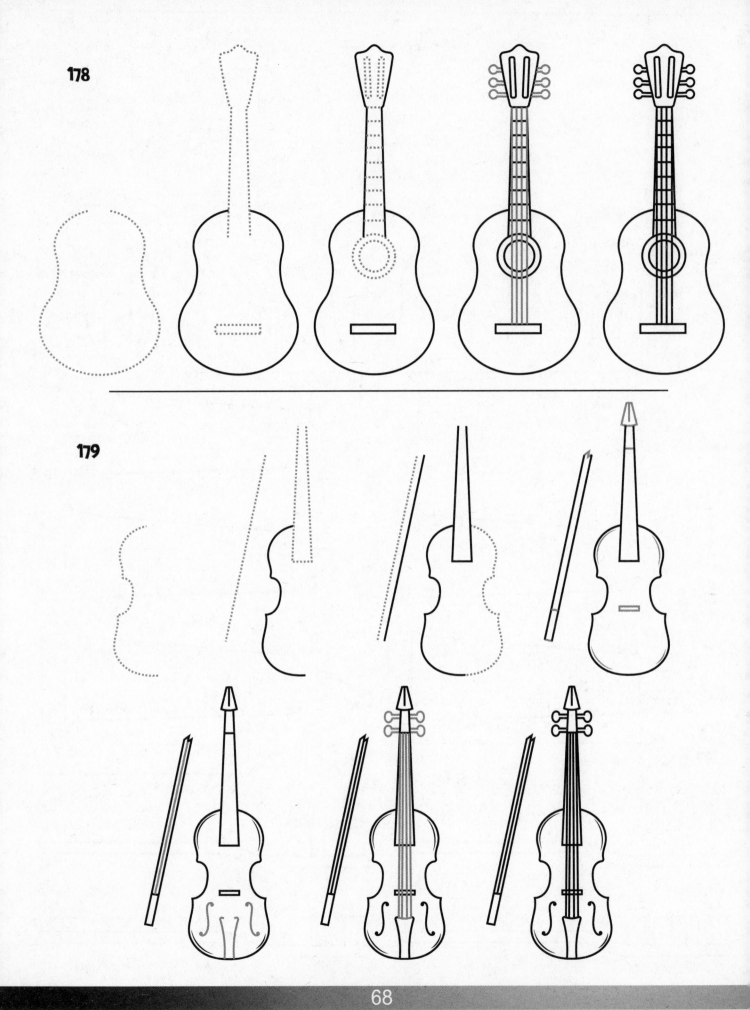

179

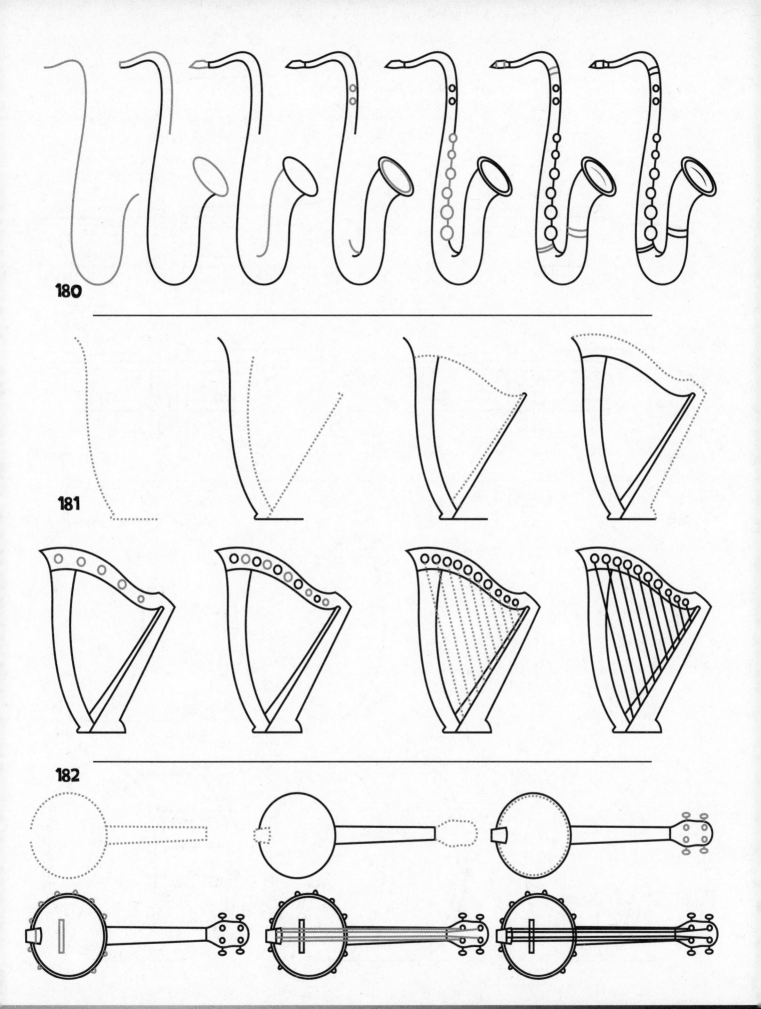

180

181

182

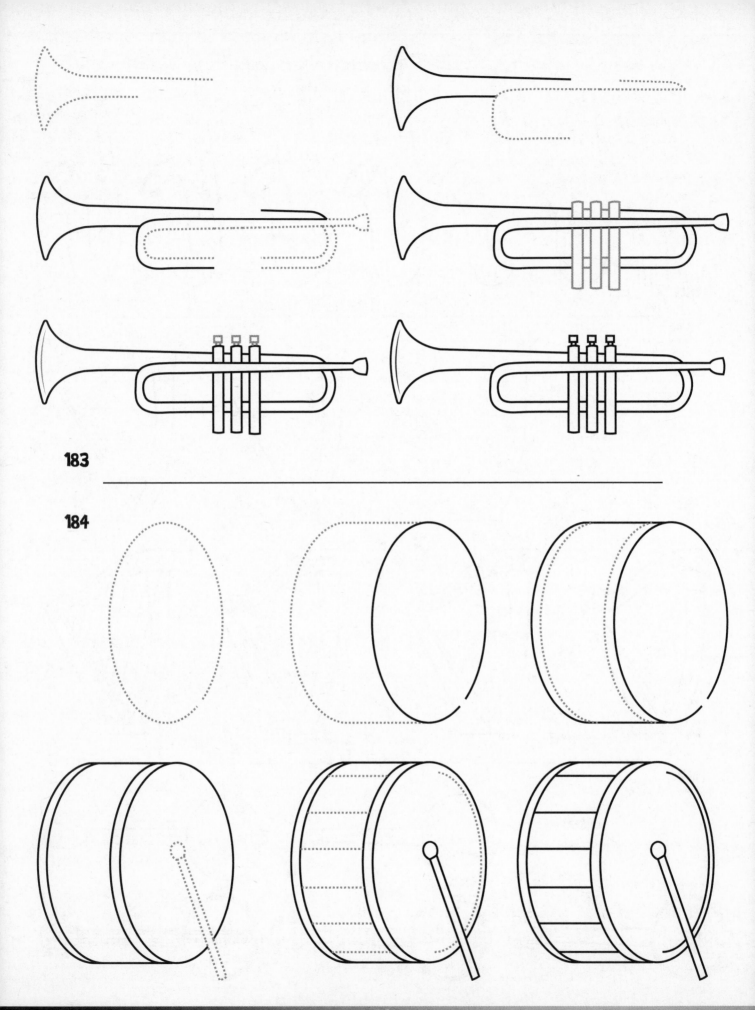

183

184

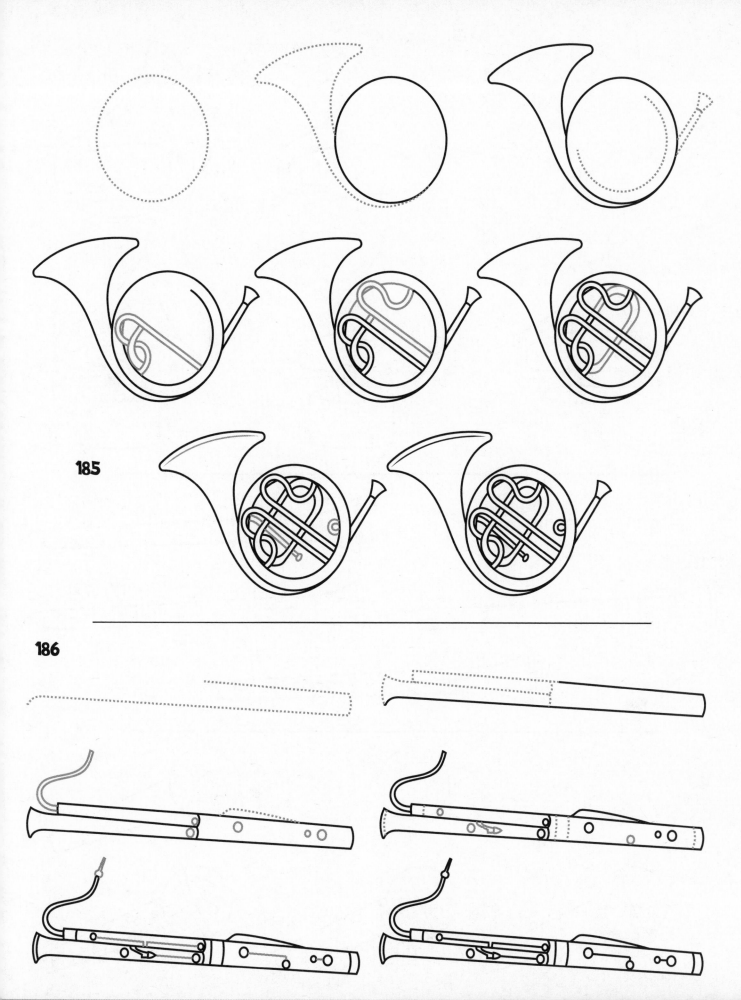

185

186

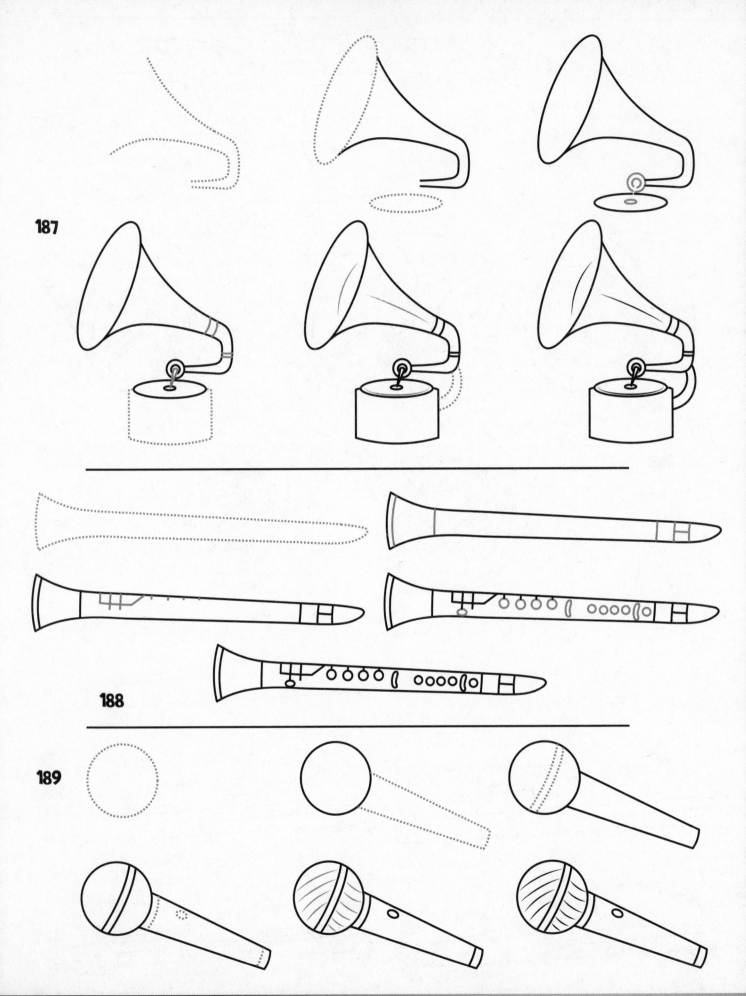

187

188

189

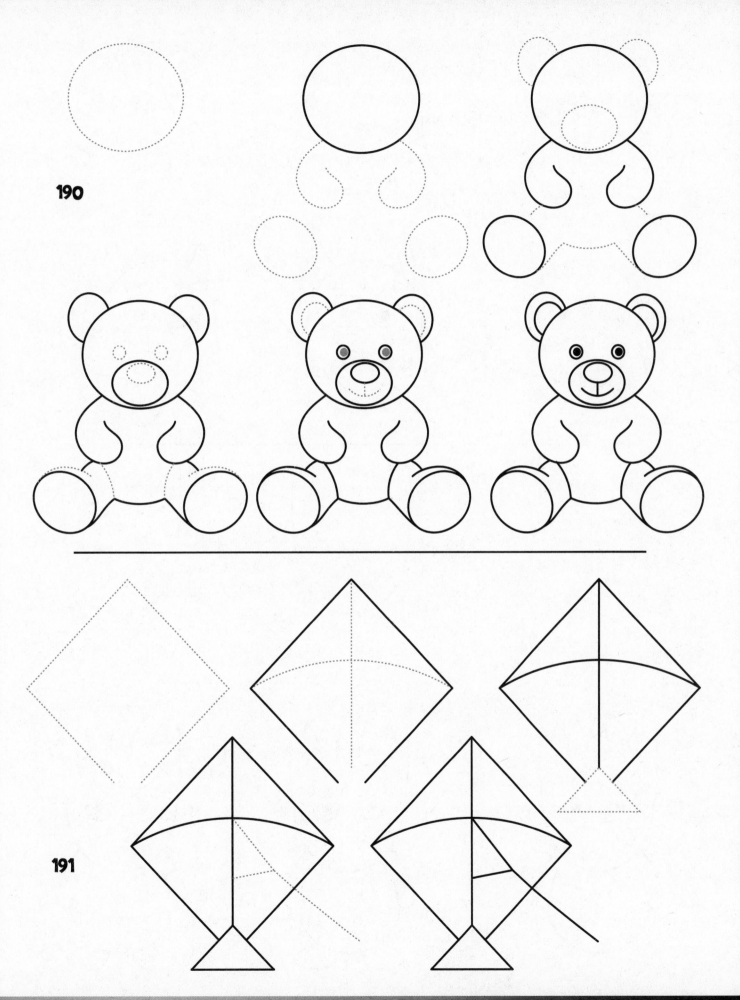

190

191

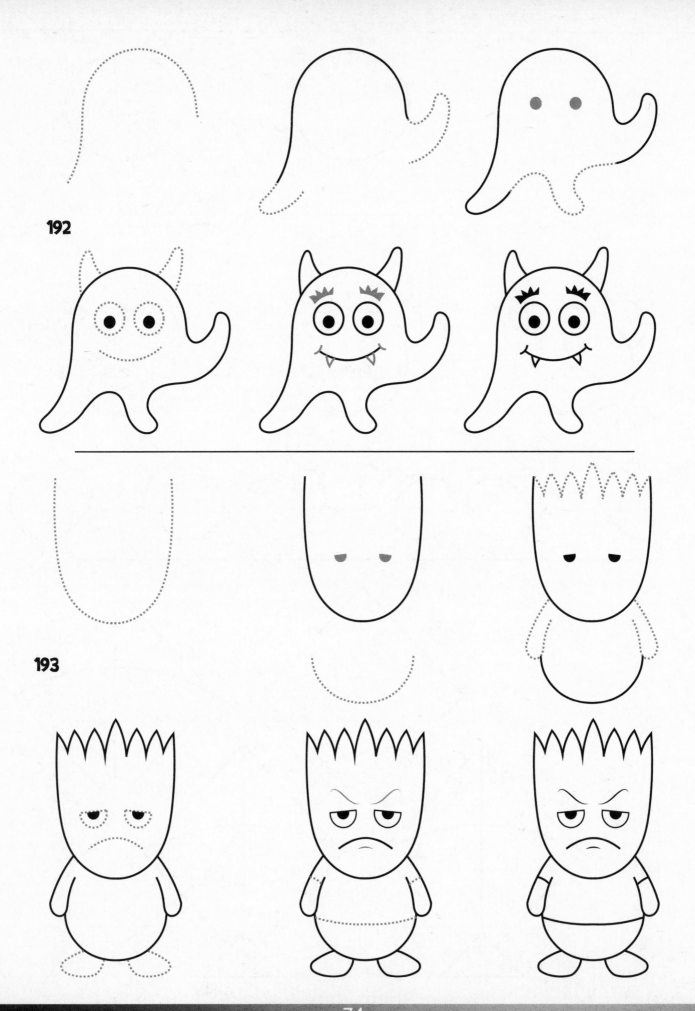

192

193

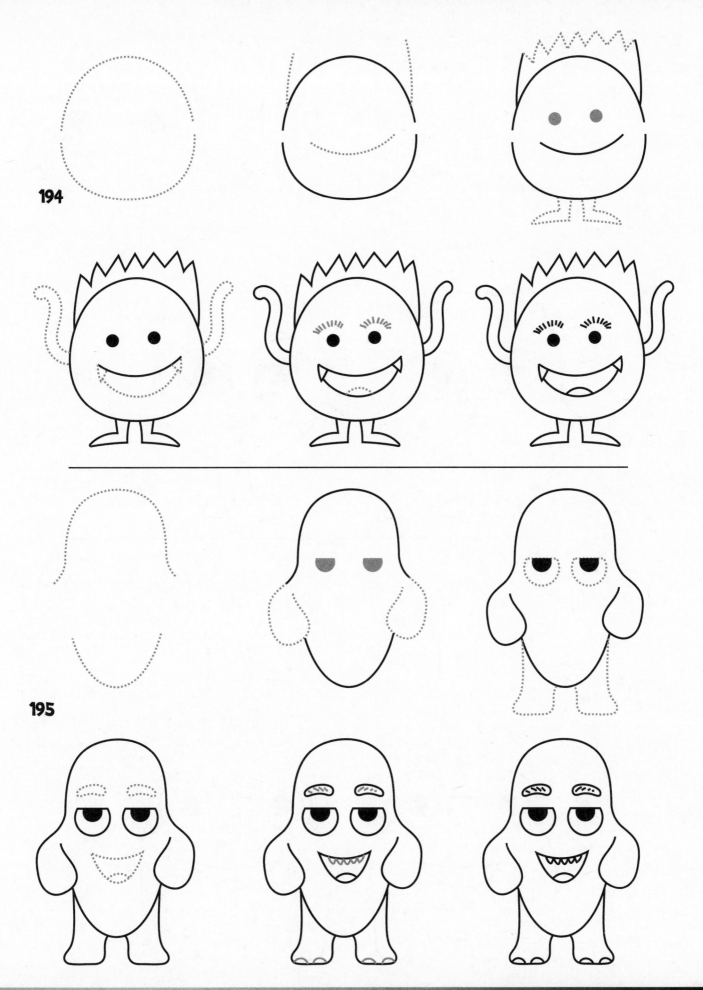

194

195

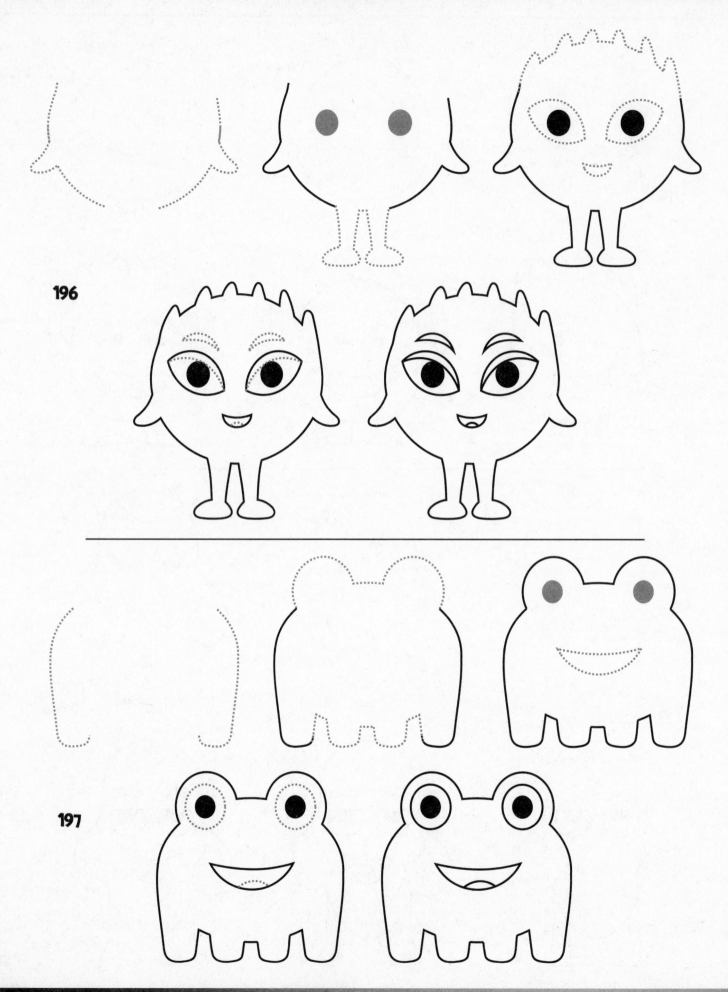

196

197

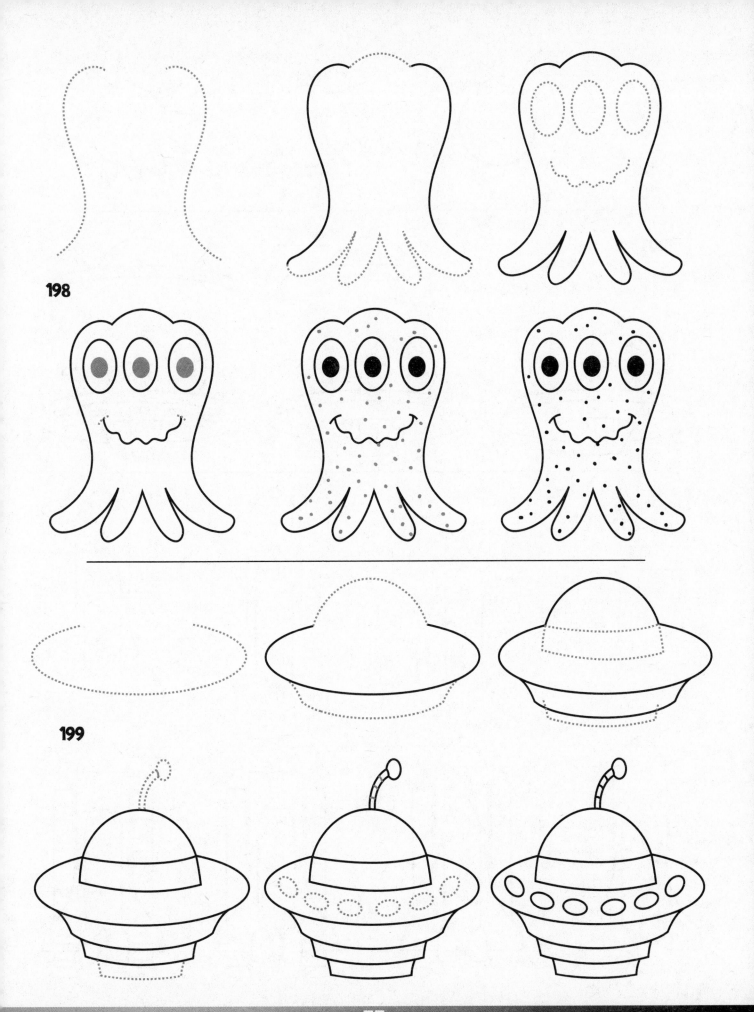

198

199

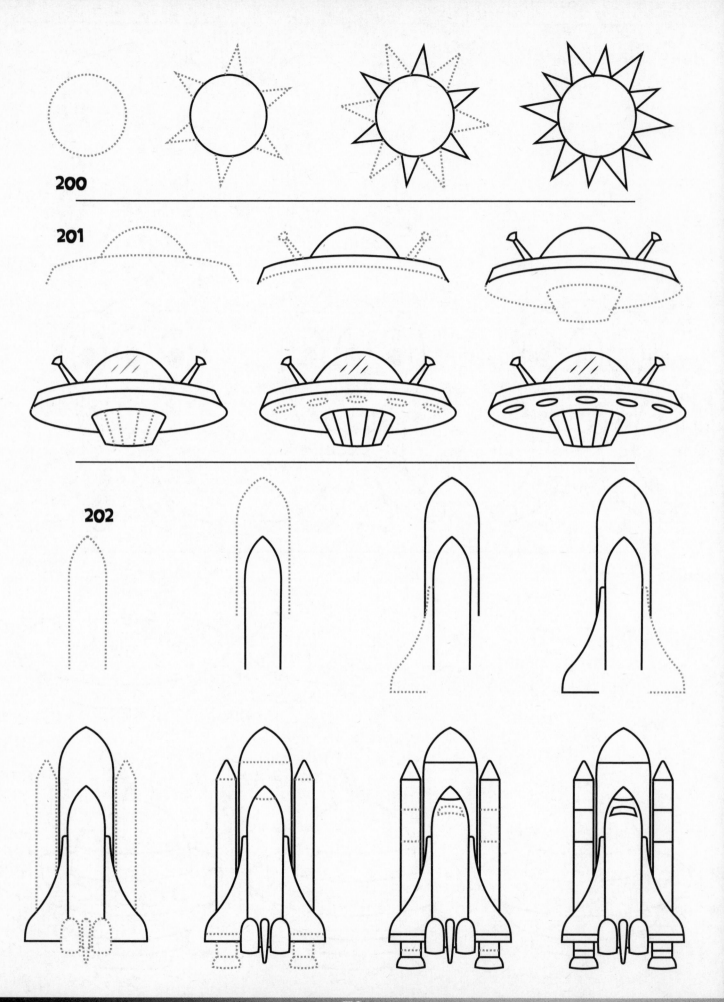

200

201

202

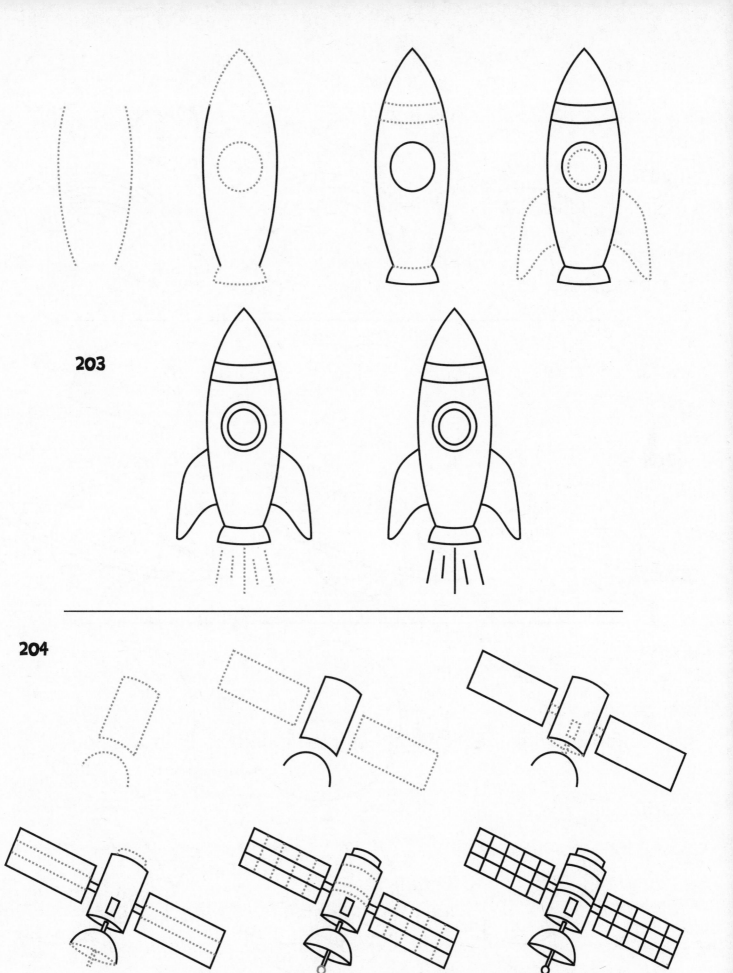

203

204

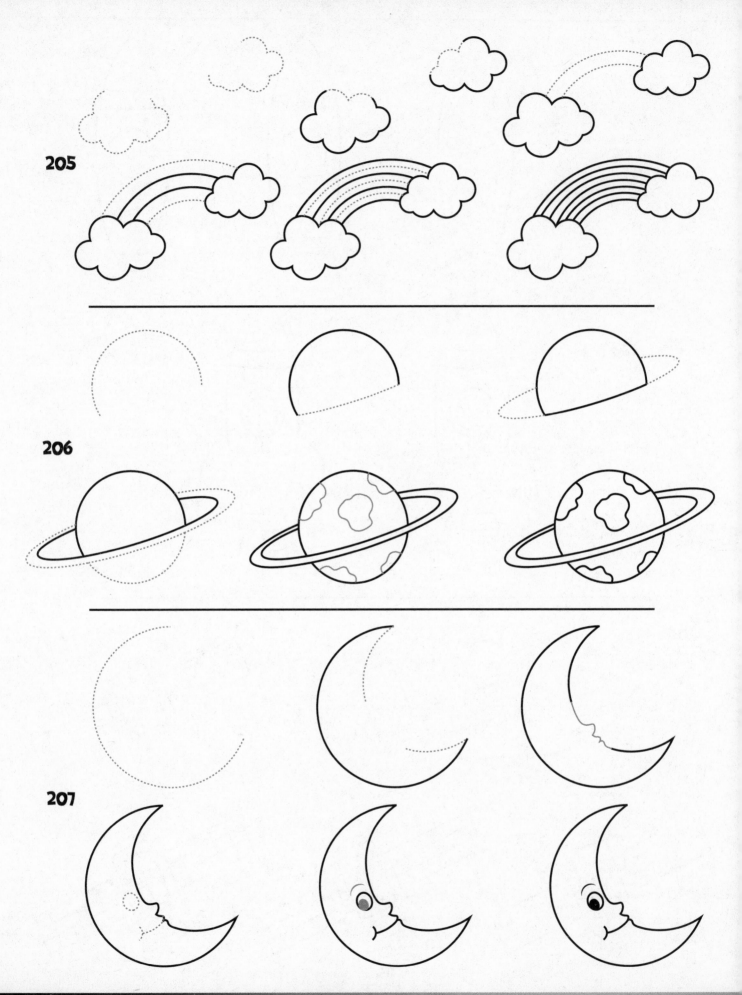

205

206

207

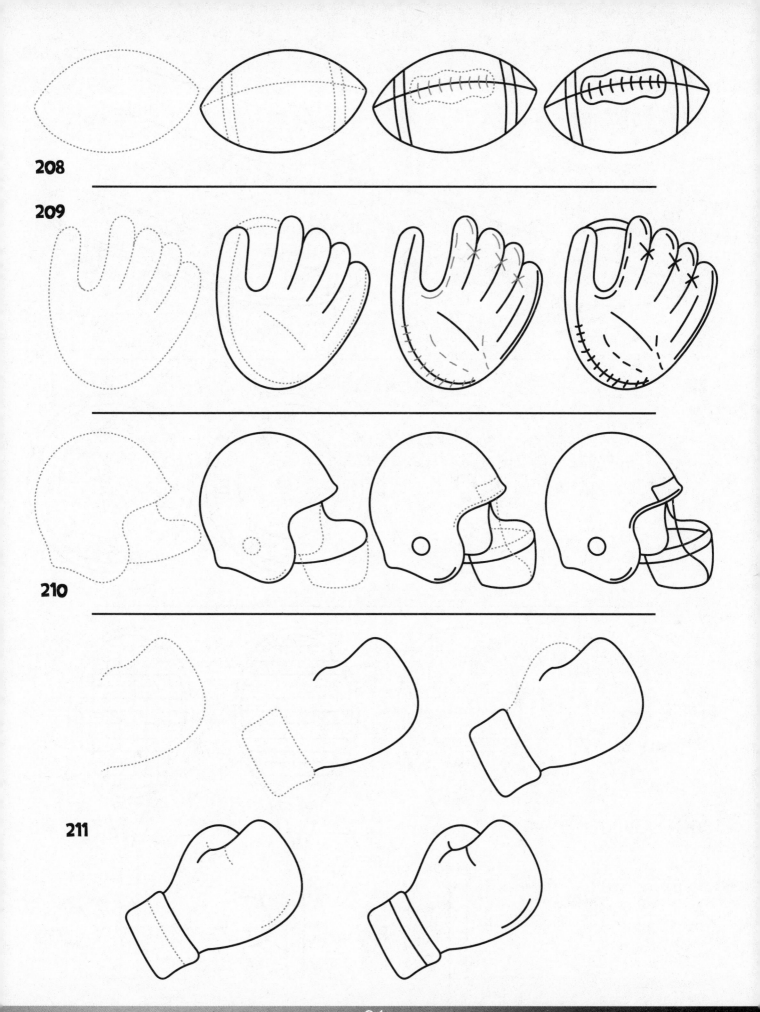

208

209

210

211

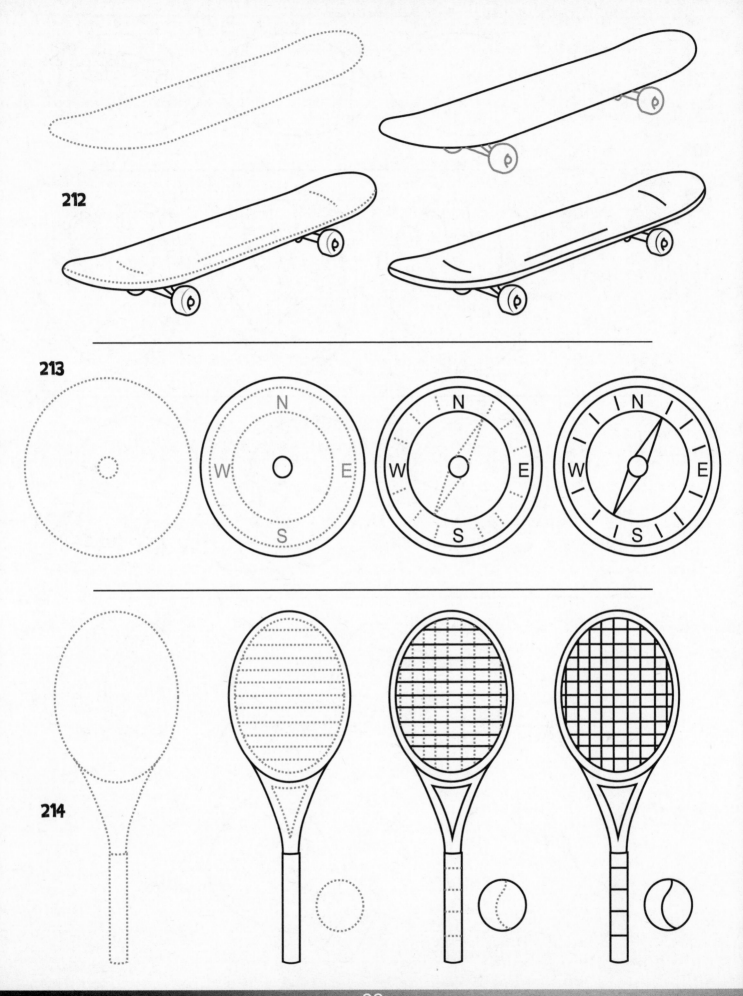

212

213

214

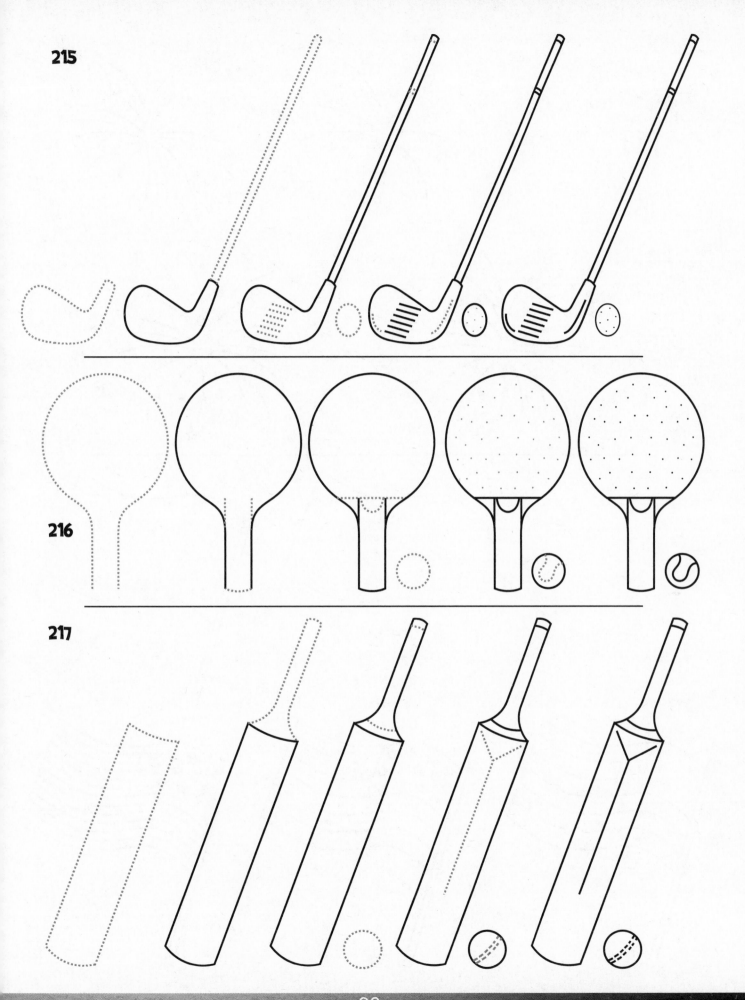

215

216

217

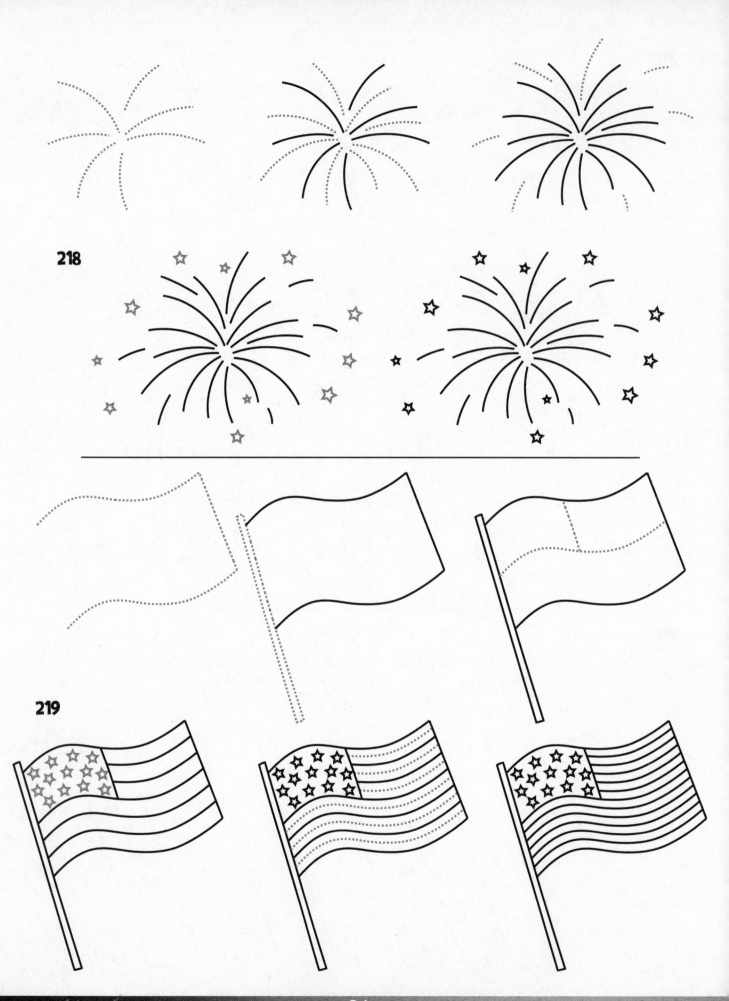

218

219

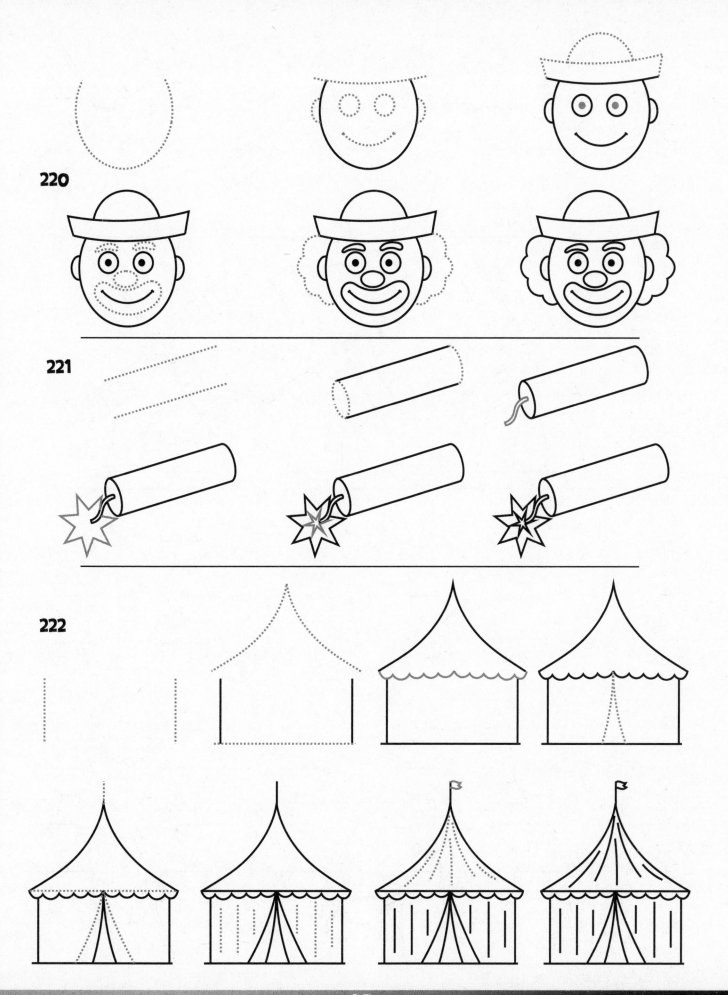

220

221

222

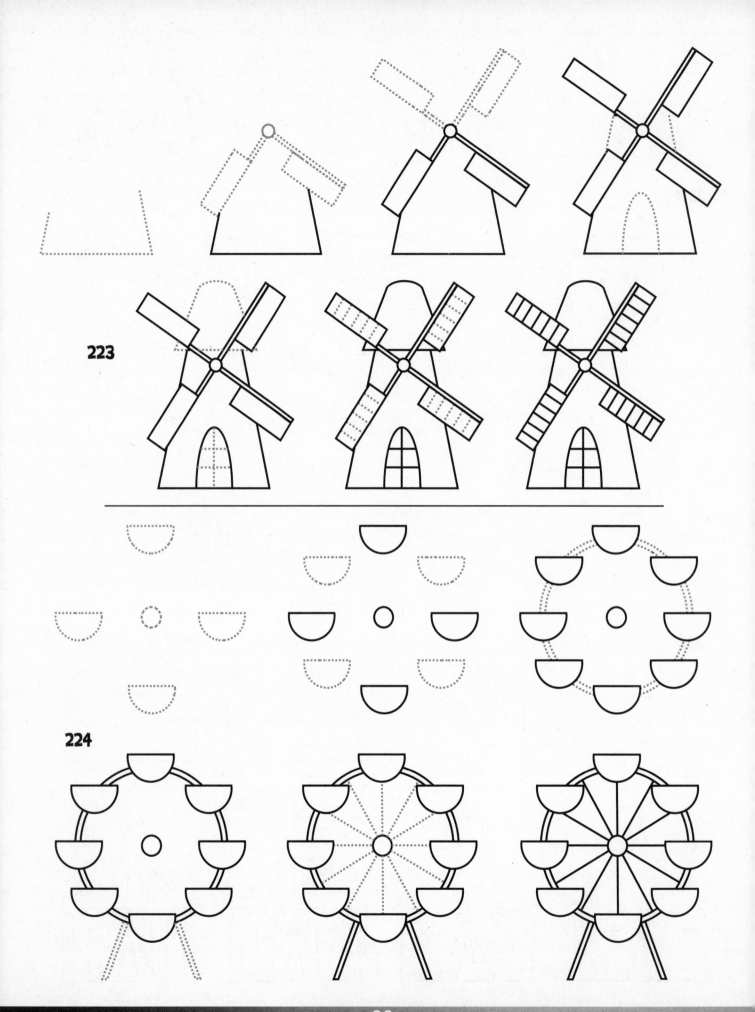

223

224

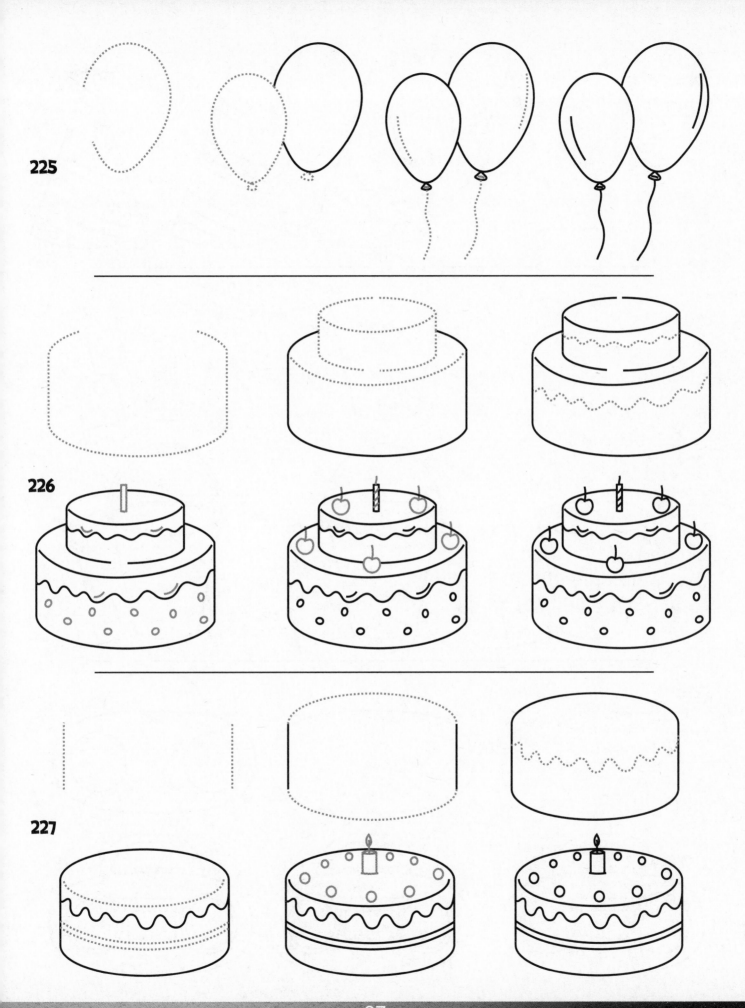

225

226

227

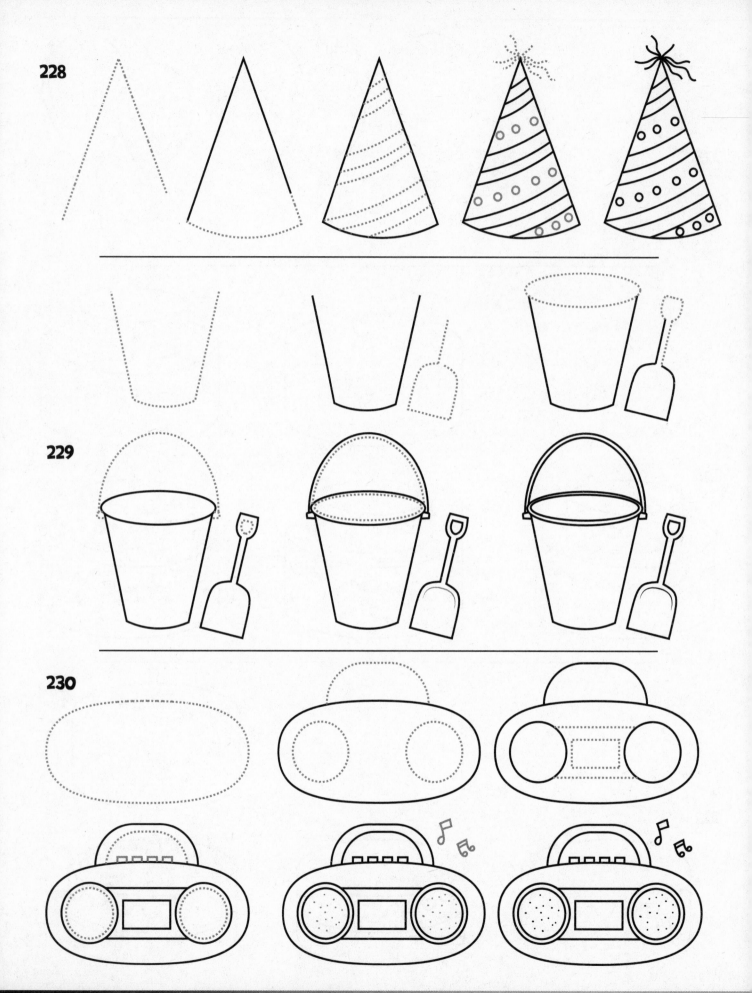

228

229

230

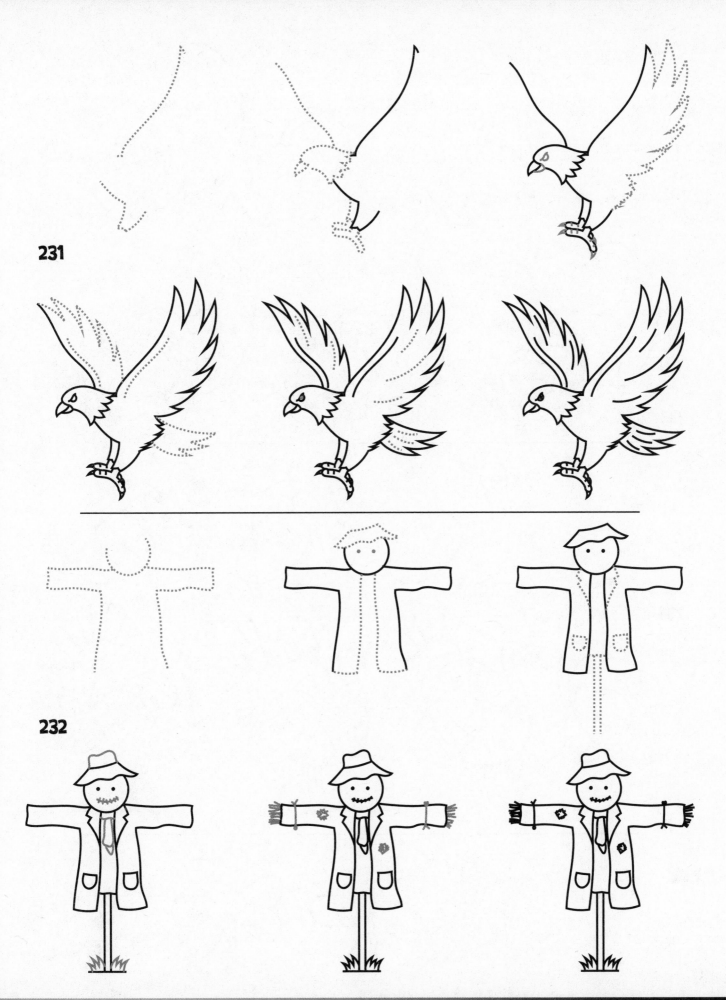

231

232

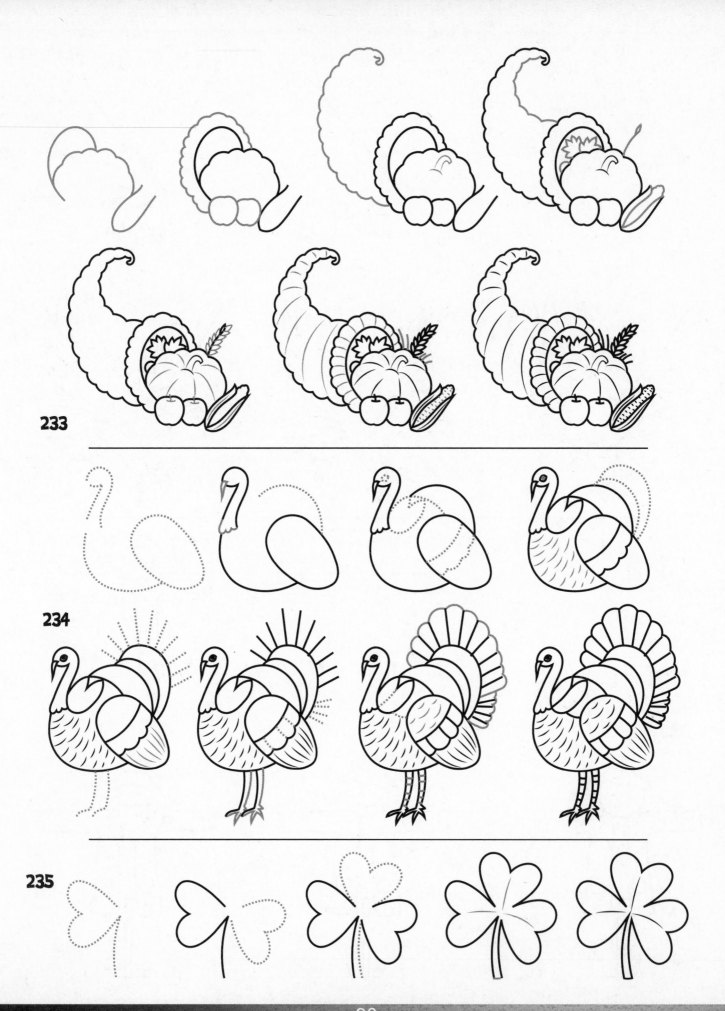

233

234

235

236

237

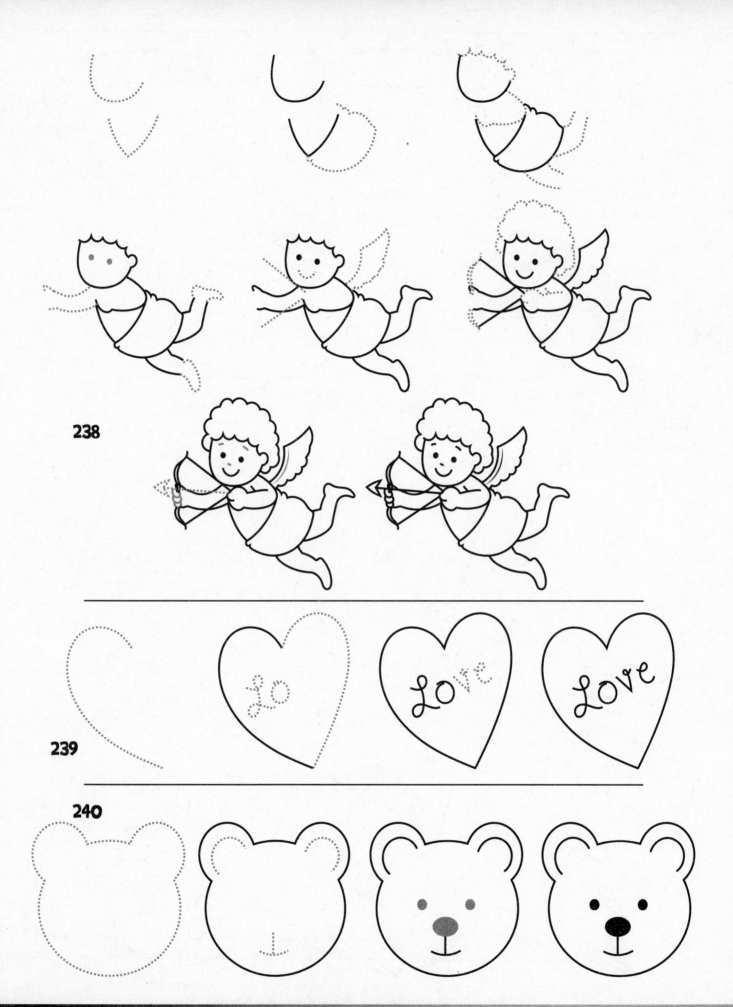

238

239

240

241

242

243

244

245

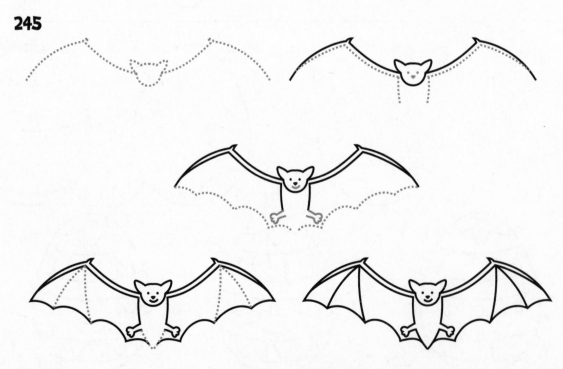

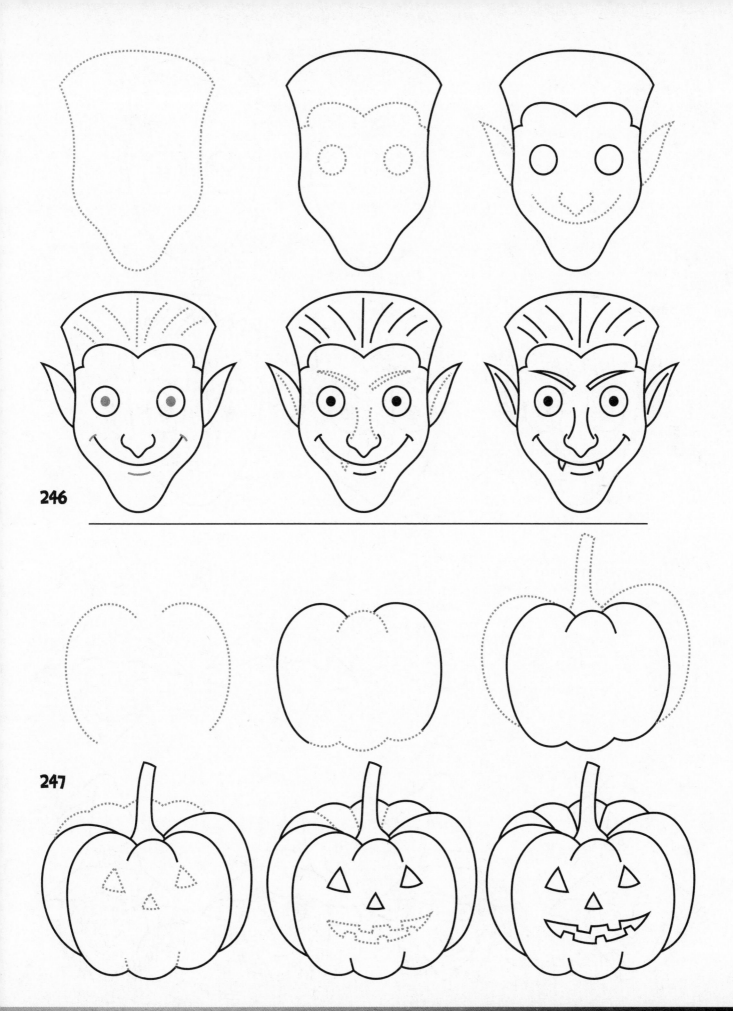

246

247

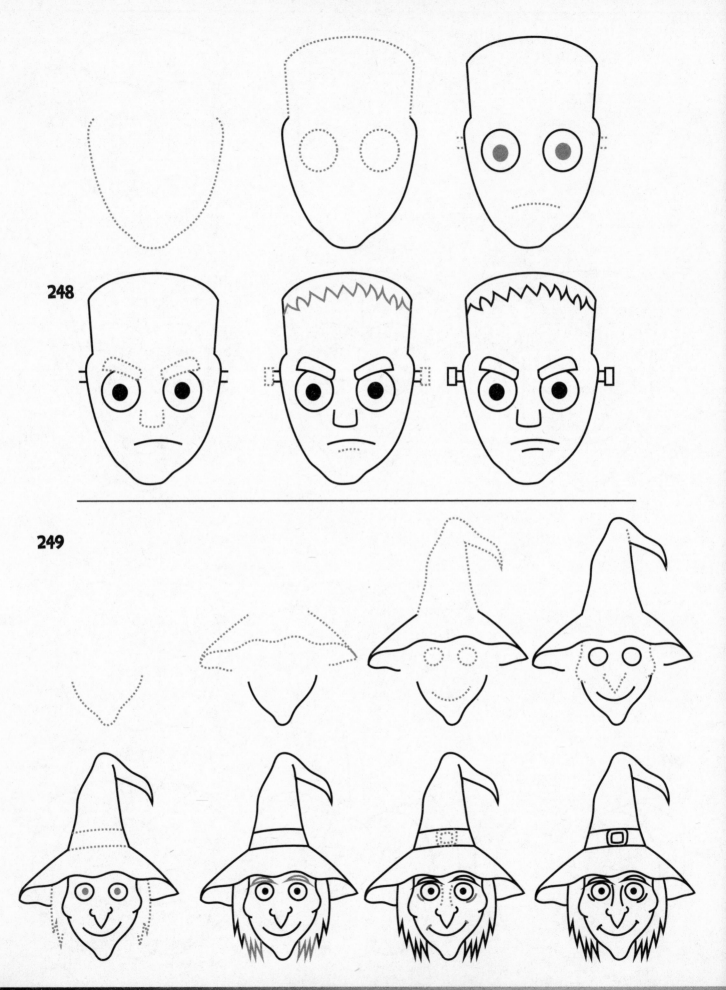

248

249

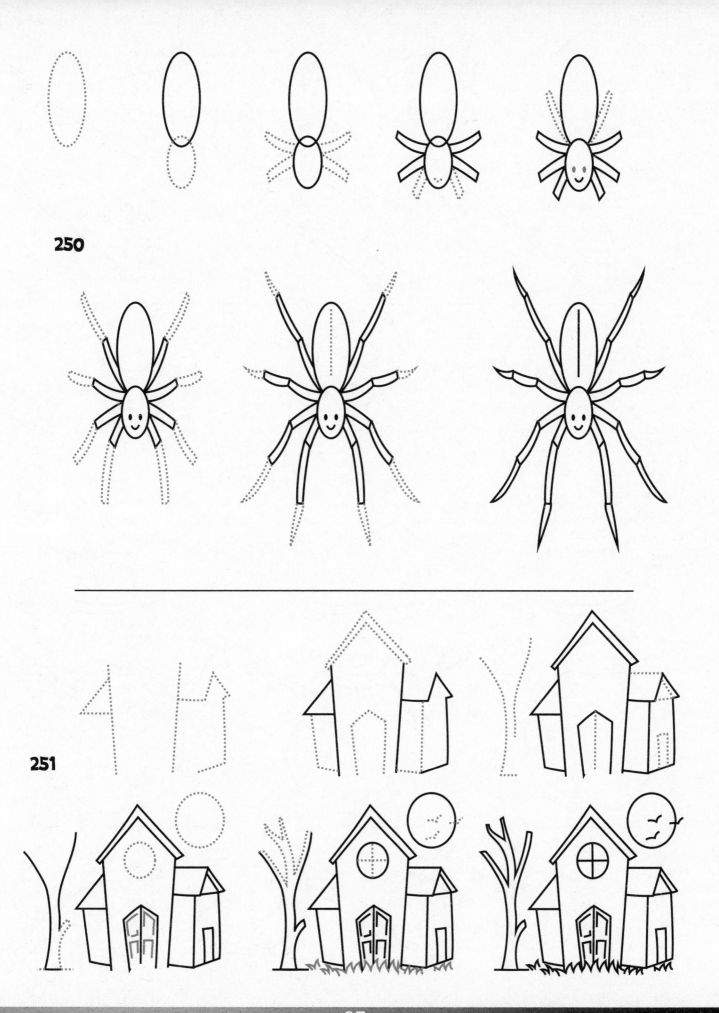

250

251

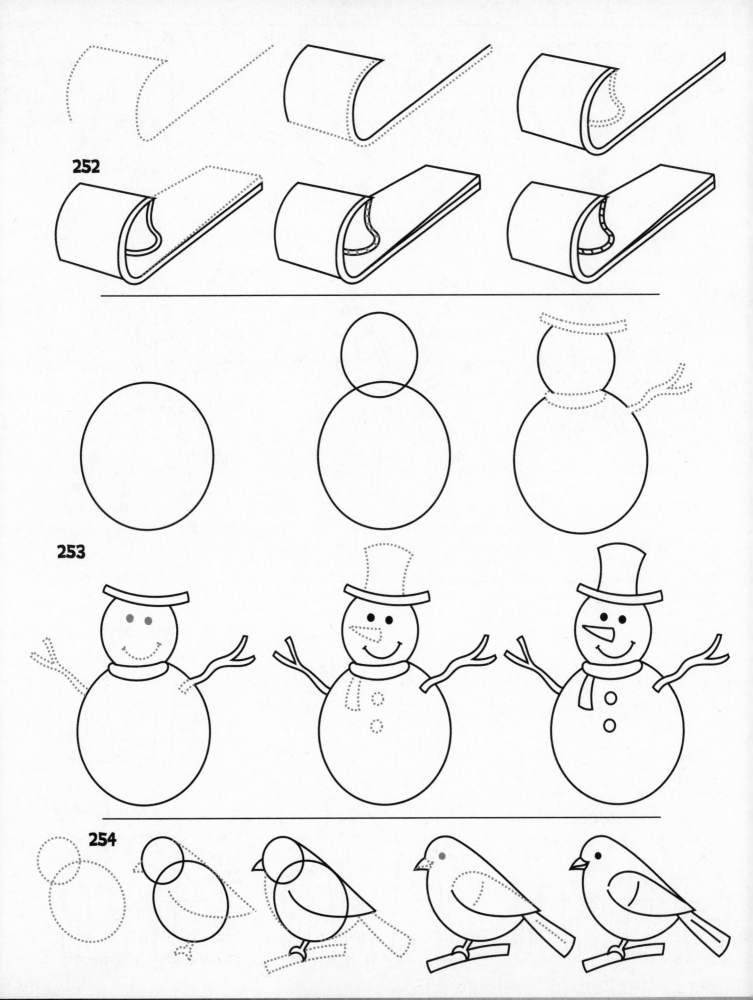

252

253

254

255

256

257

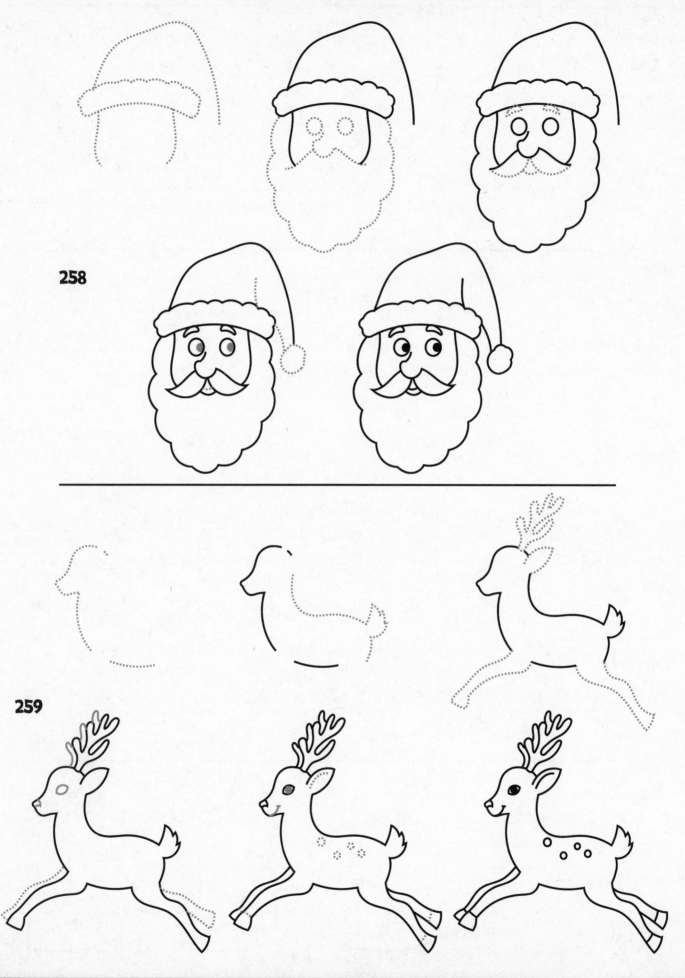

258

259

260

261

262

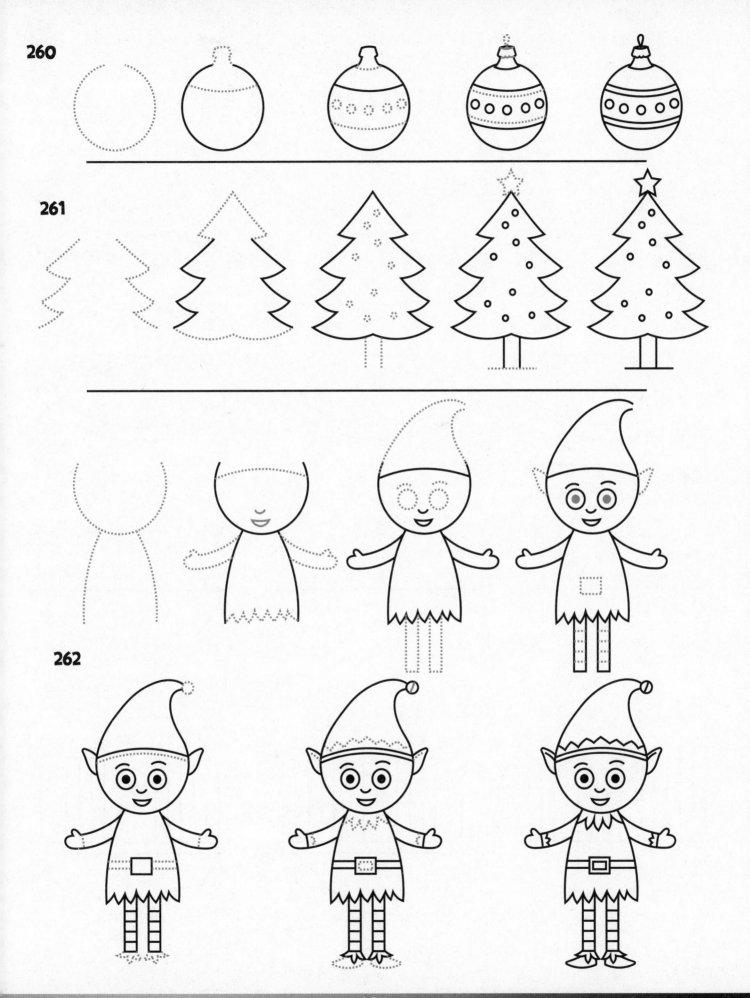

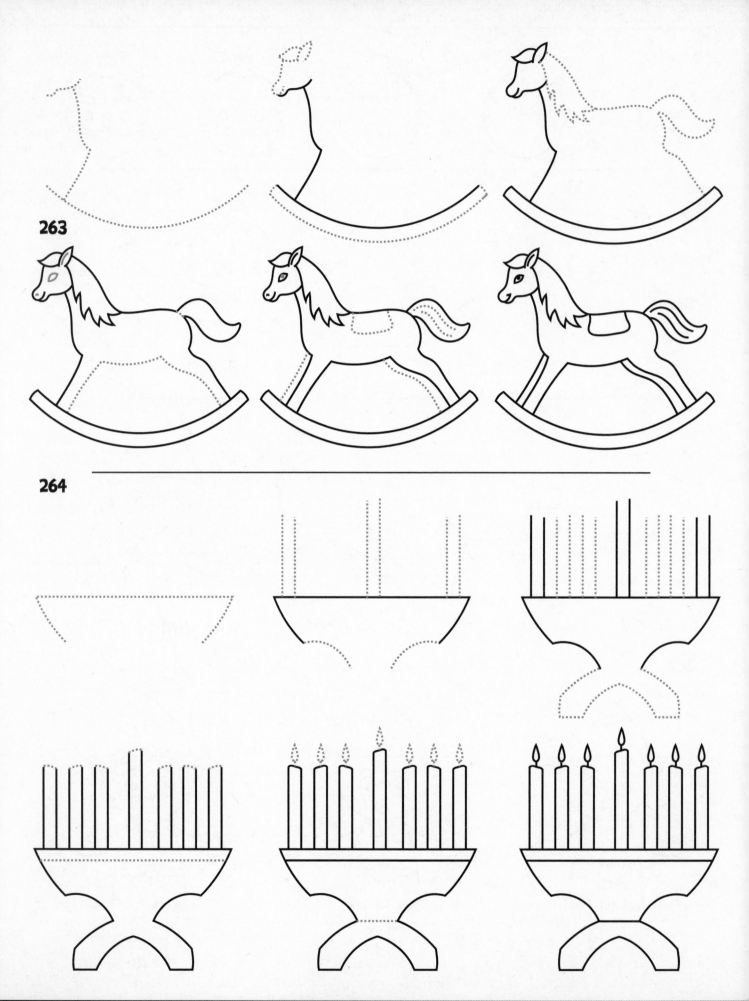

263

264

265

266

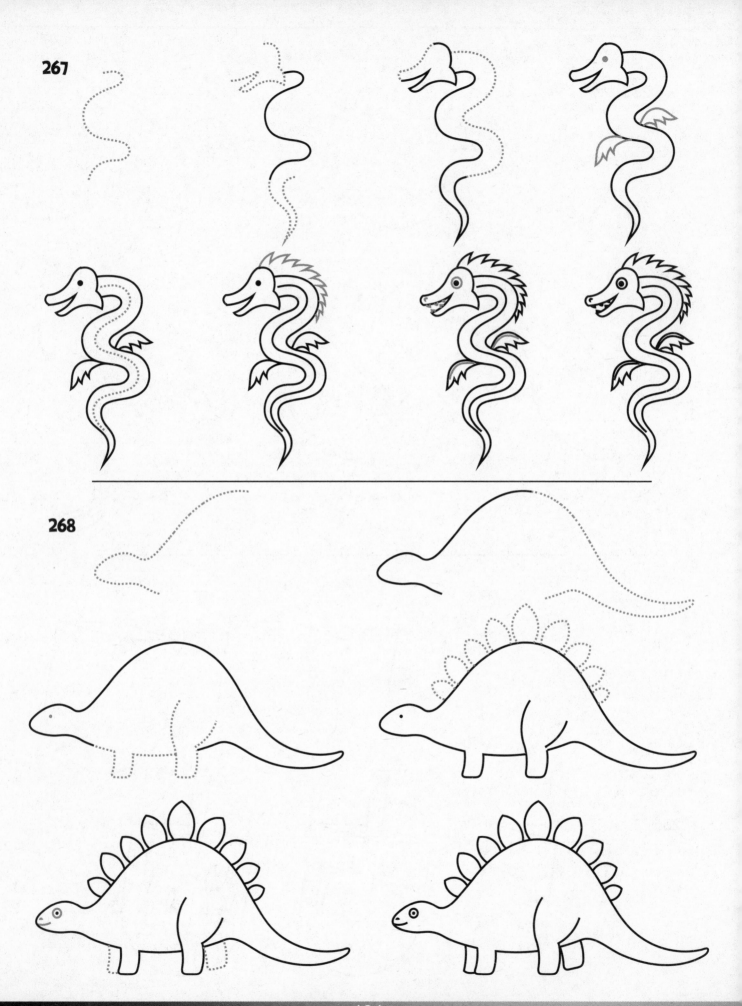

267

268

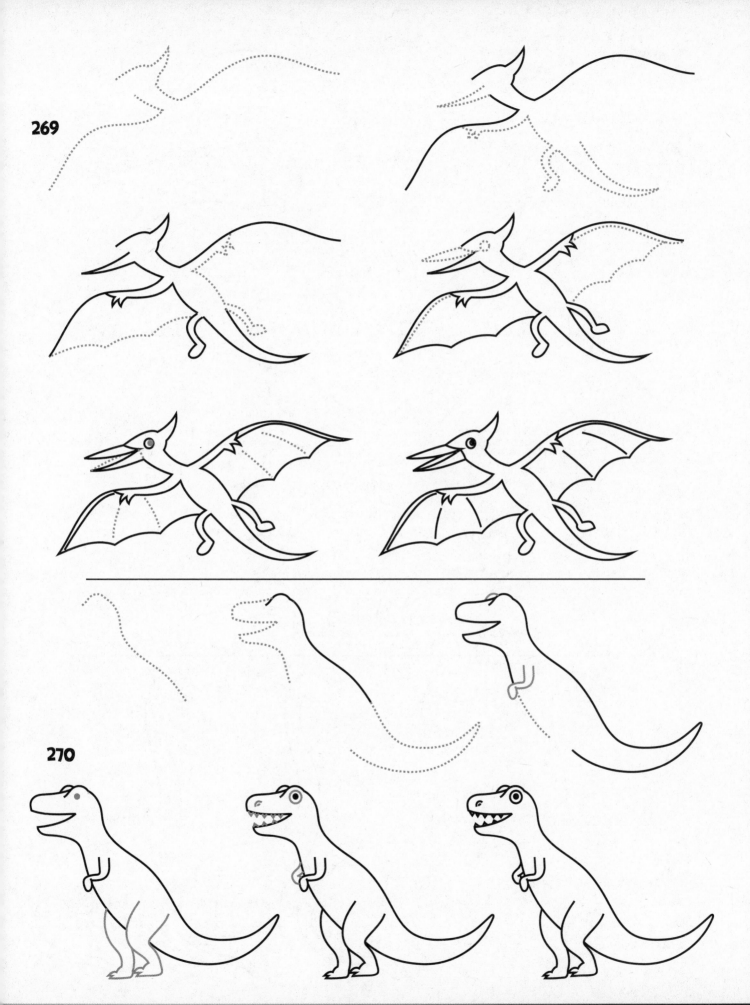

269

270

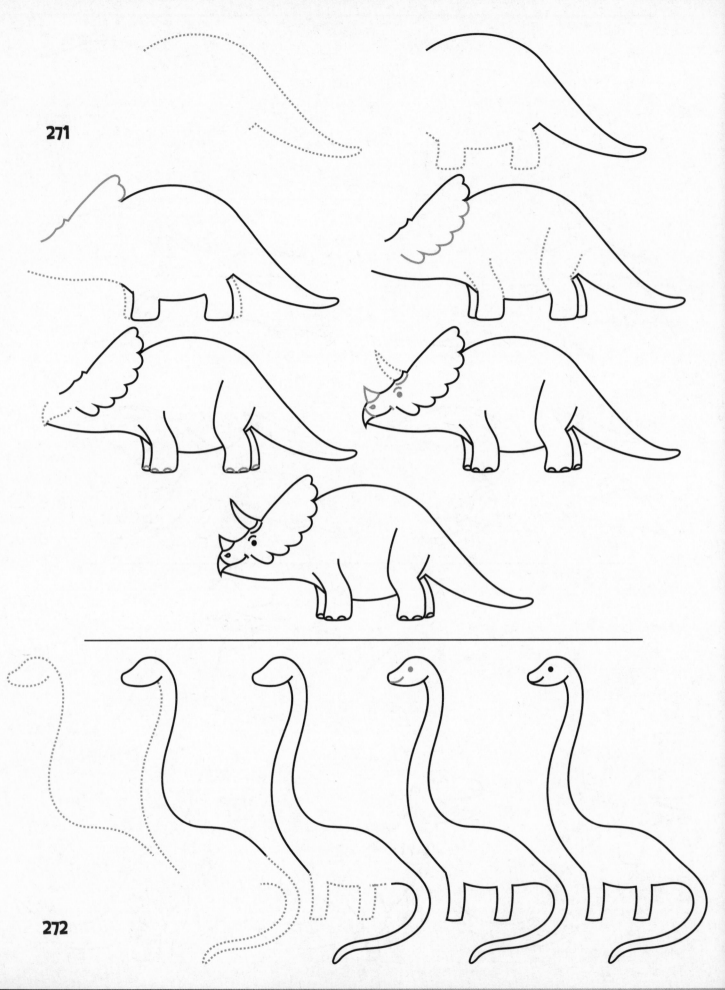

271

272

273

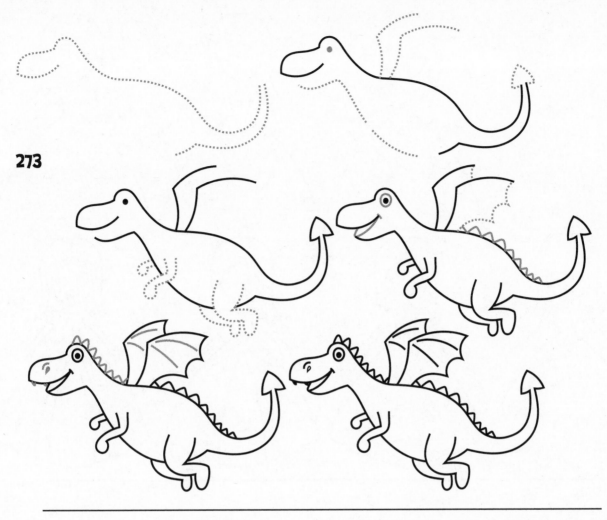

274

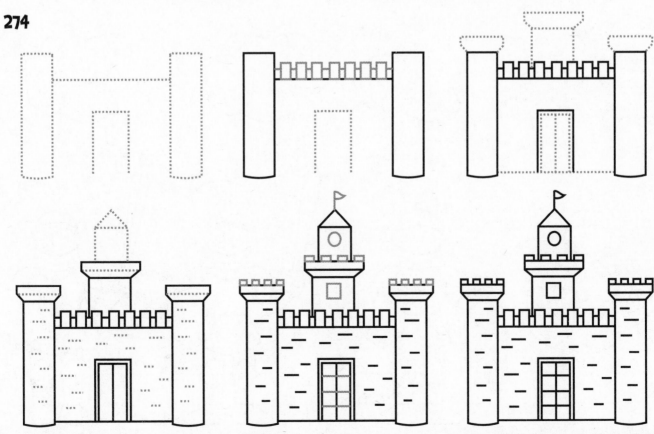

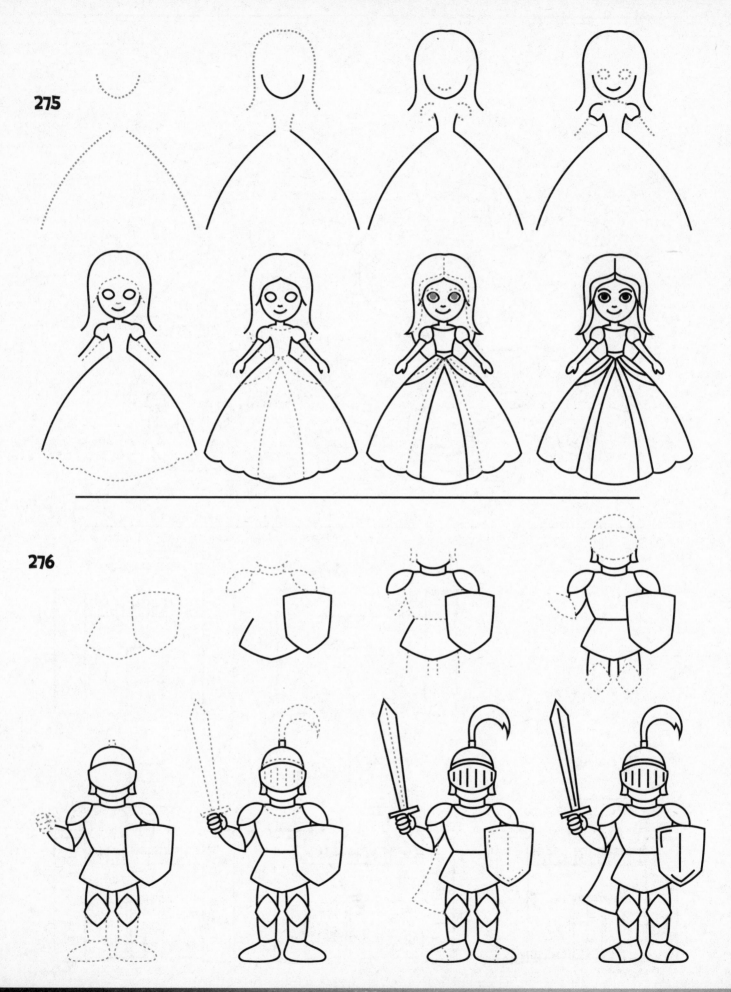

275

276

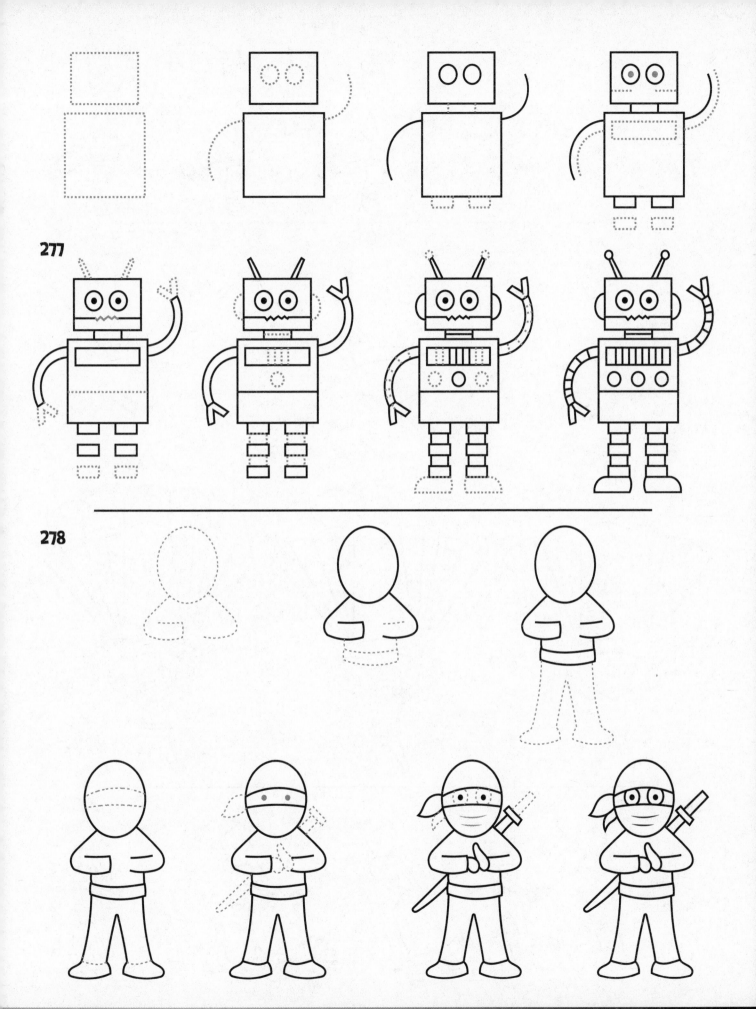

277

278

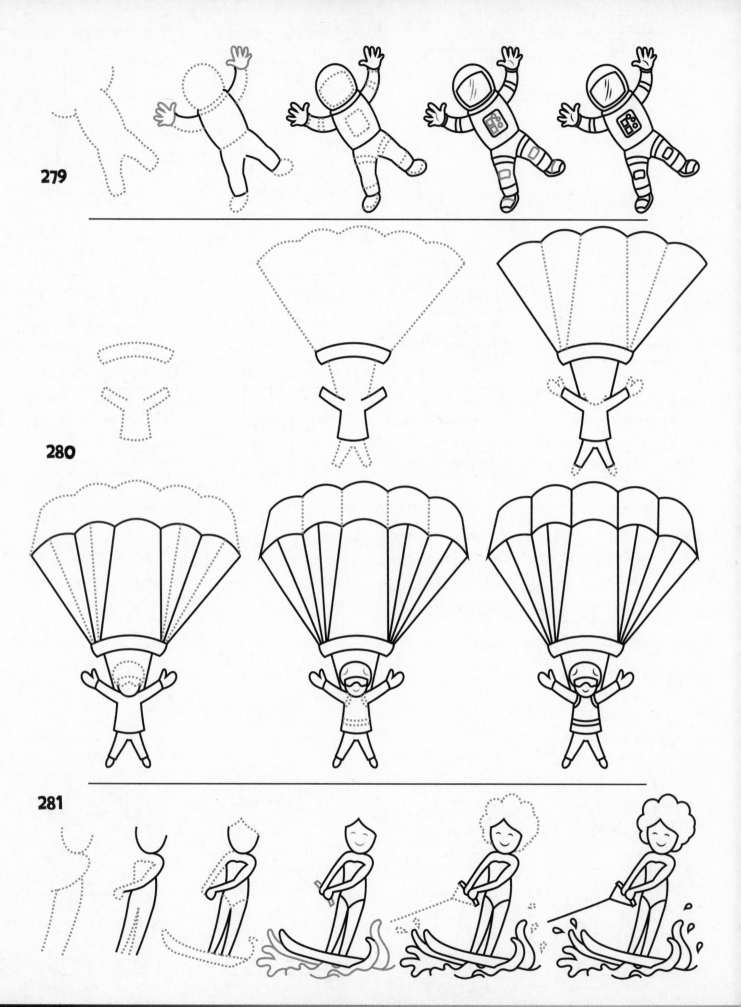

279

280

281

282

283

111

286

287

288

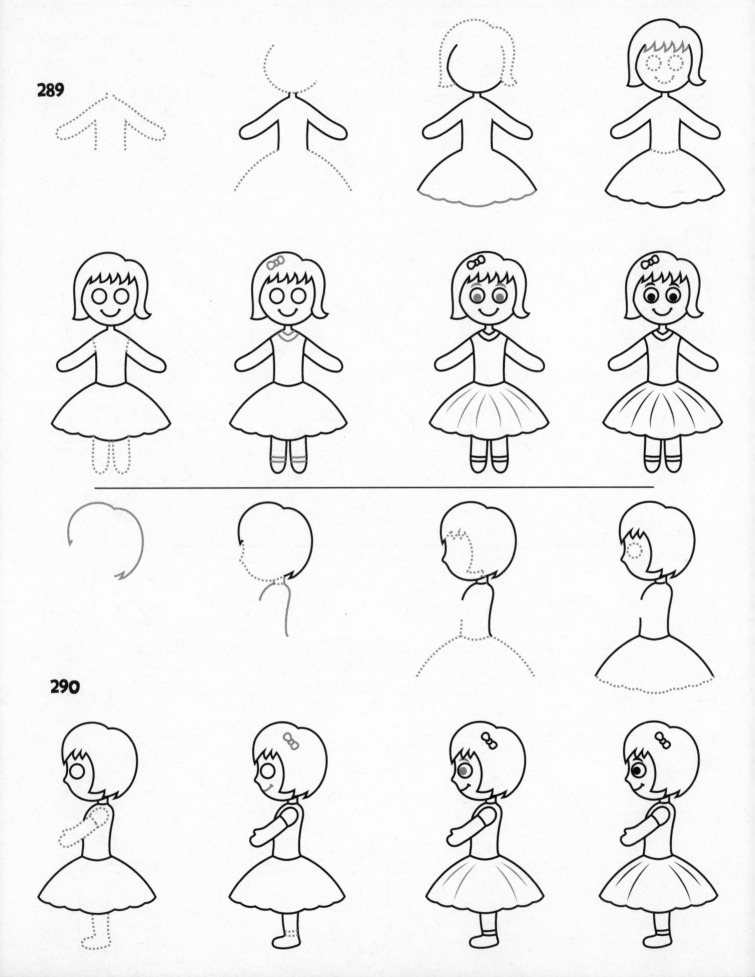

289

290

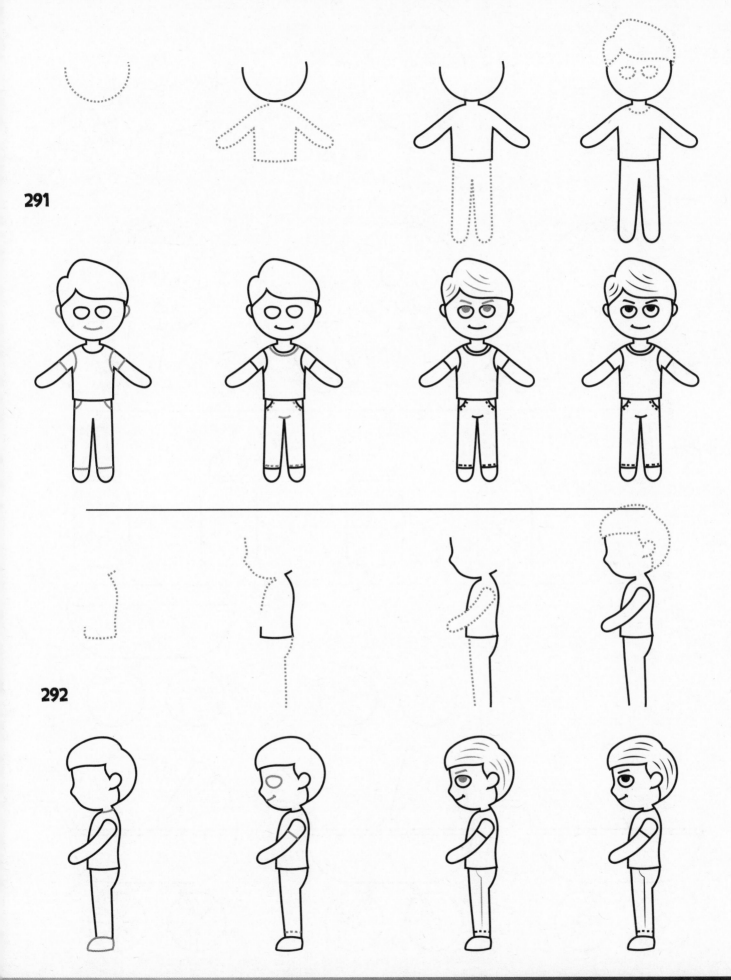

291

292

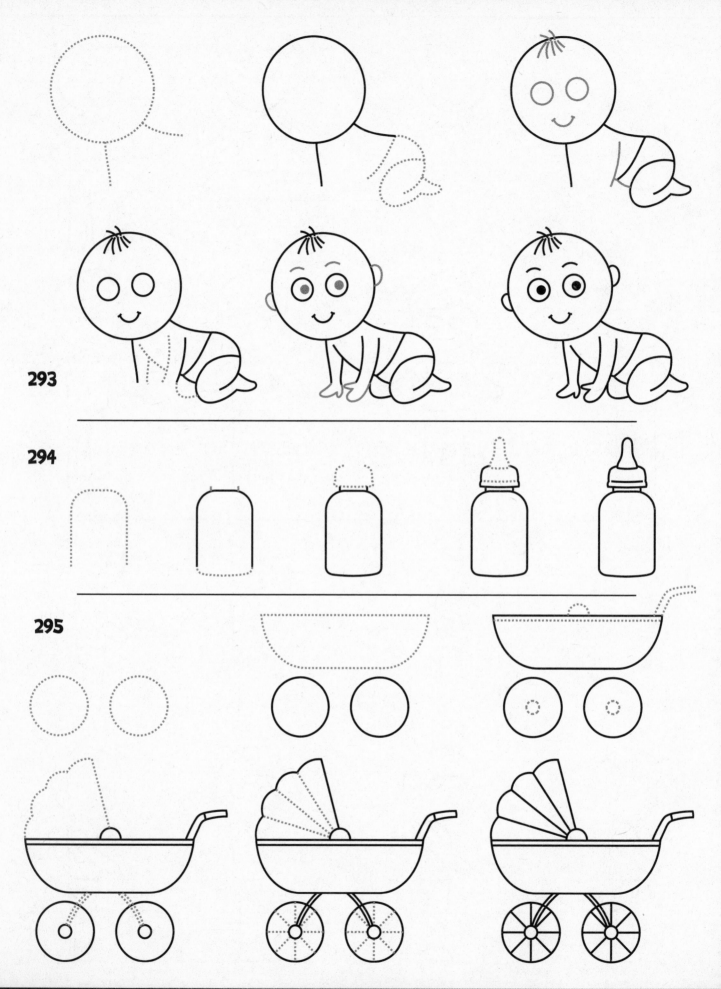

293

294

295

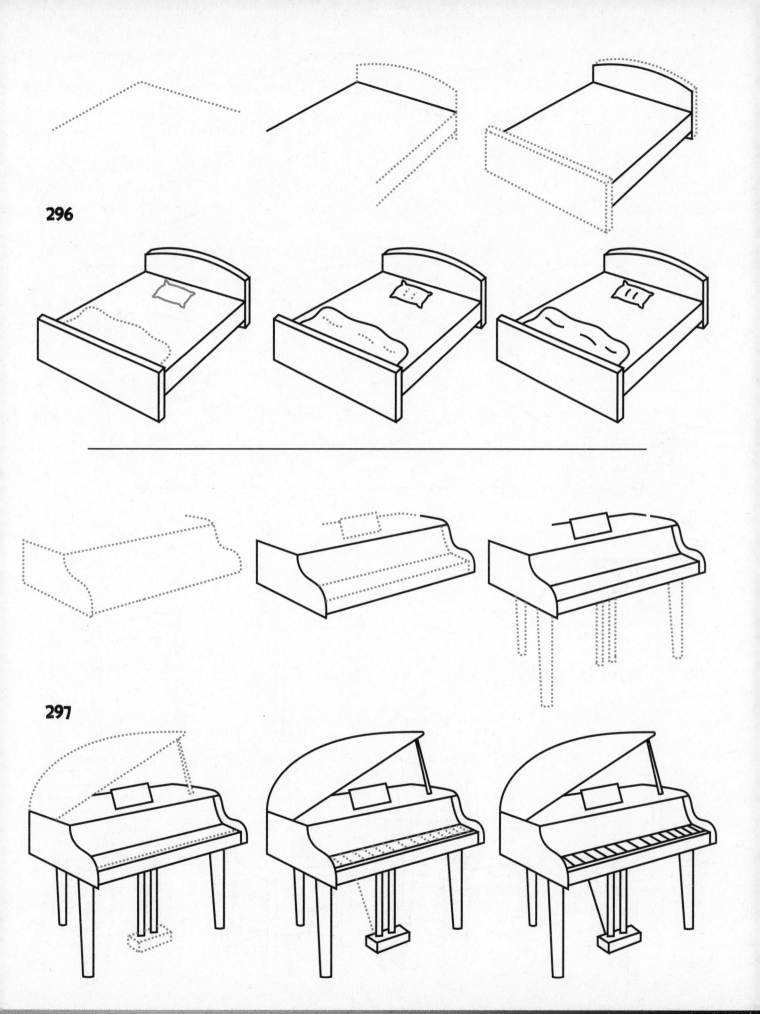

296

297

298

299

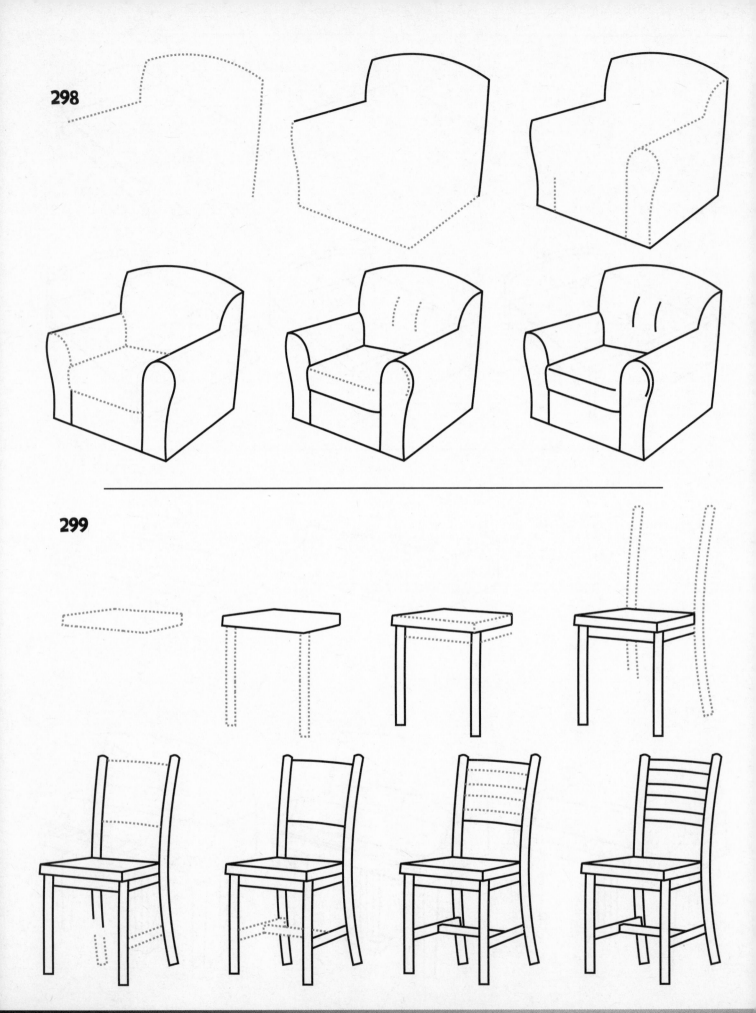

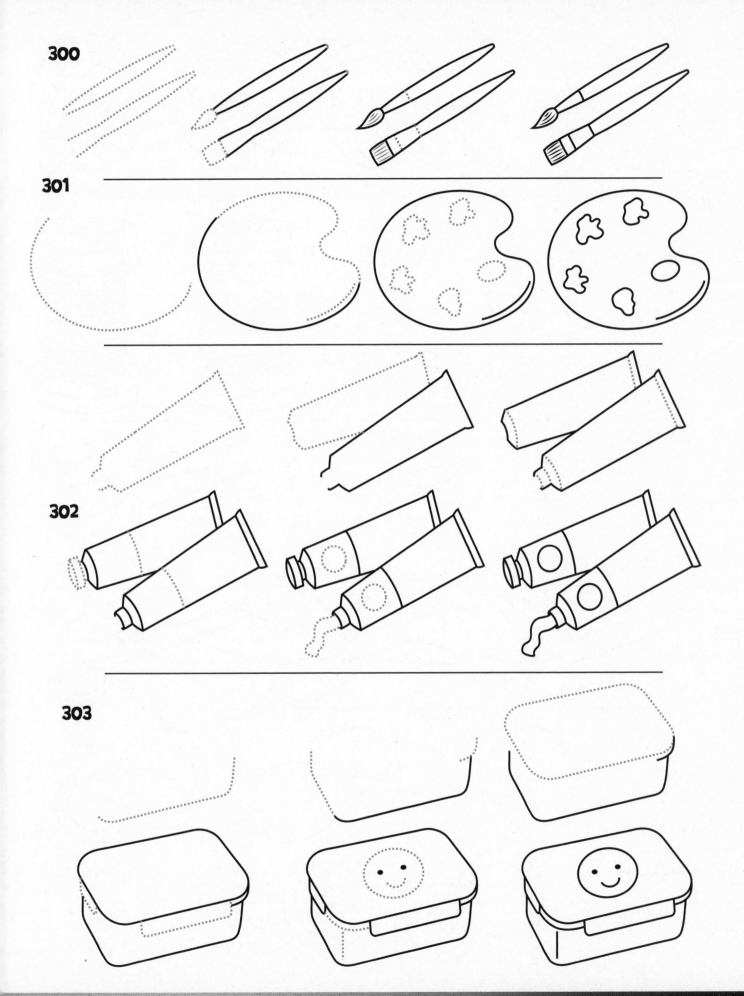

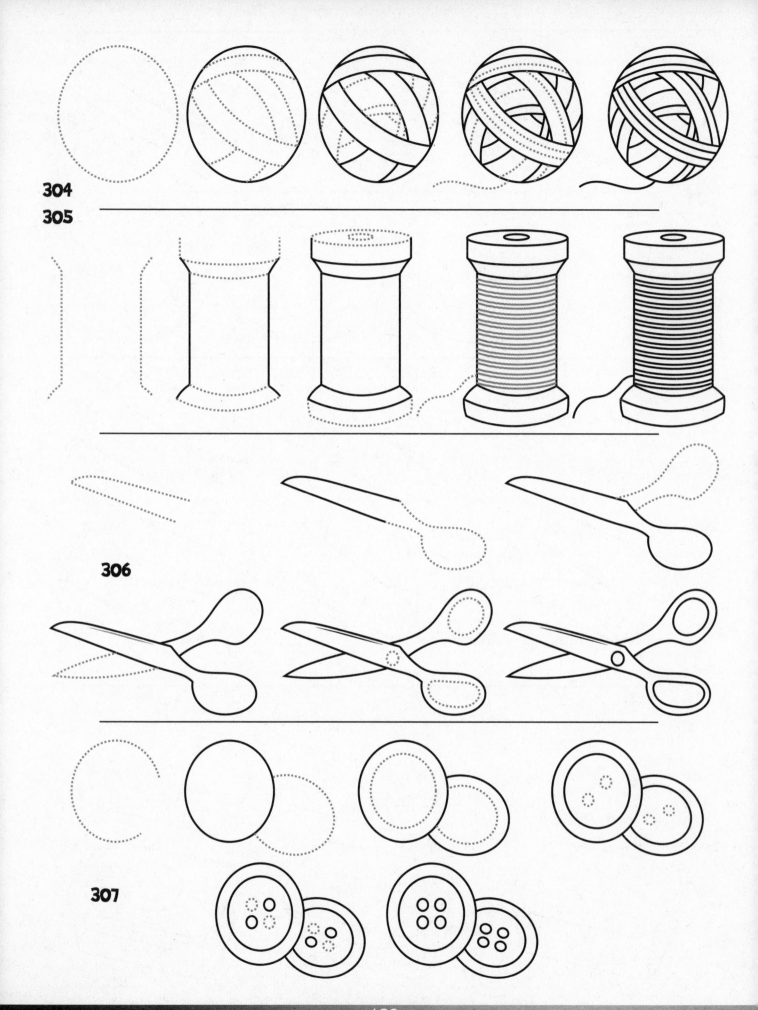

304

305

306

307

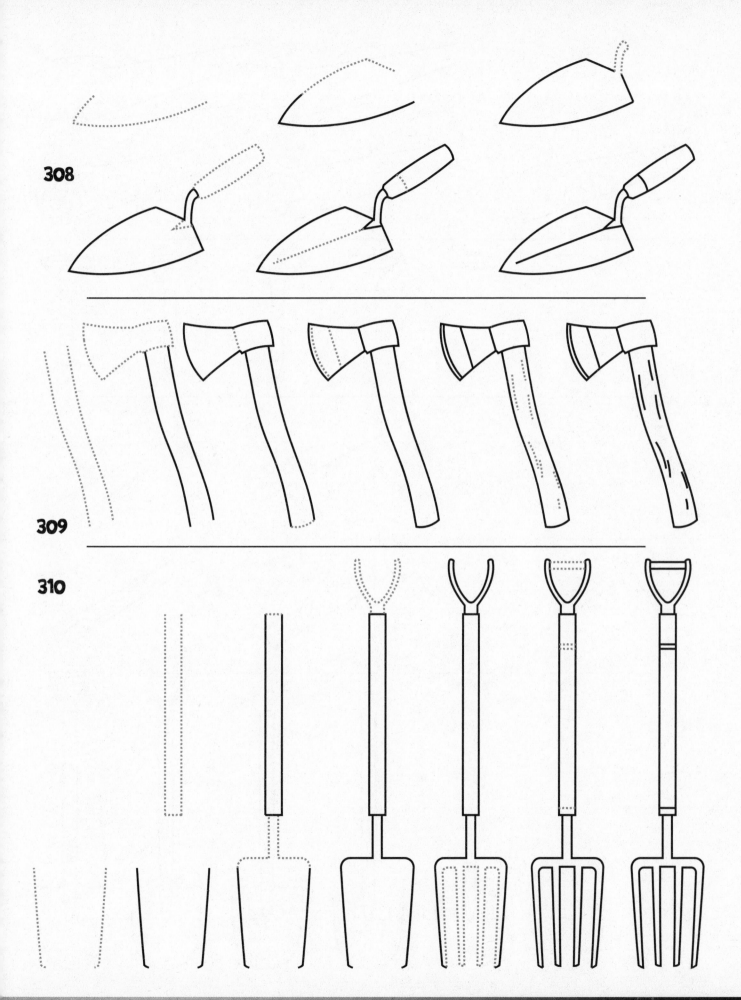

308

309

310

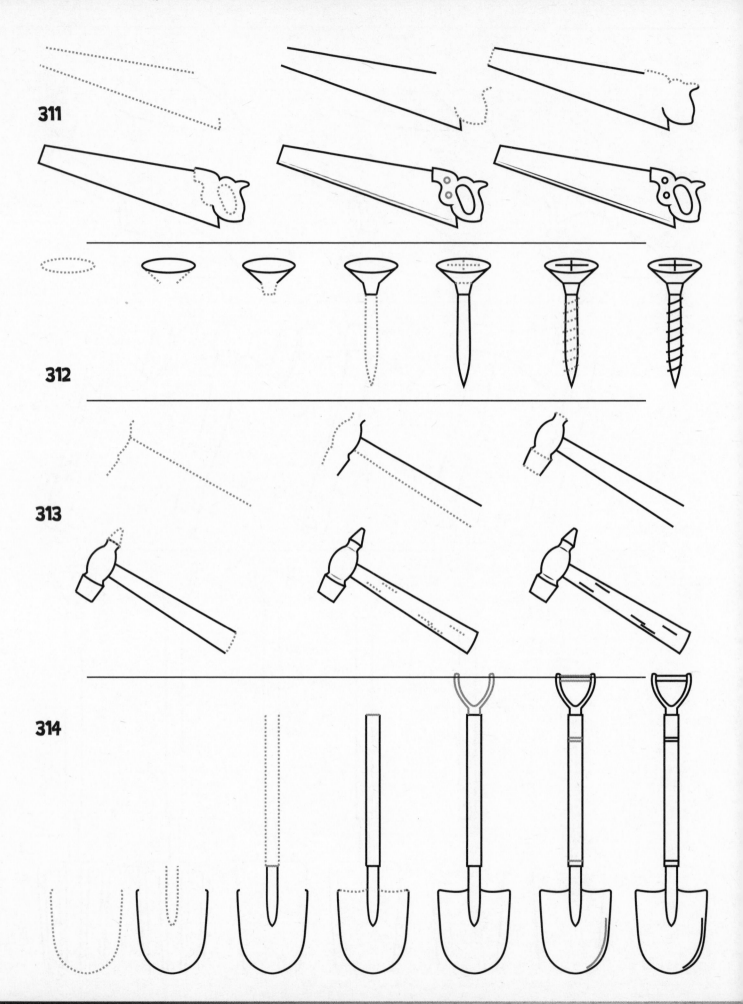

311

312

313

314

315

316

317

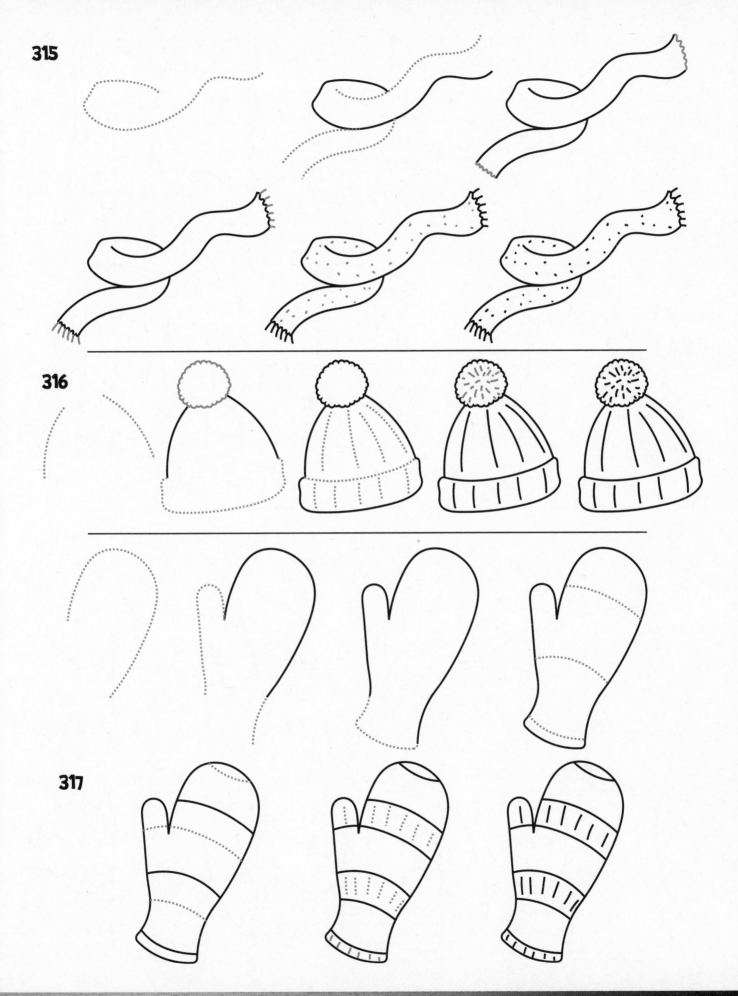

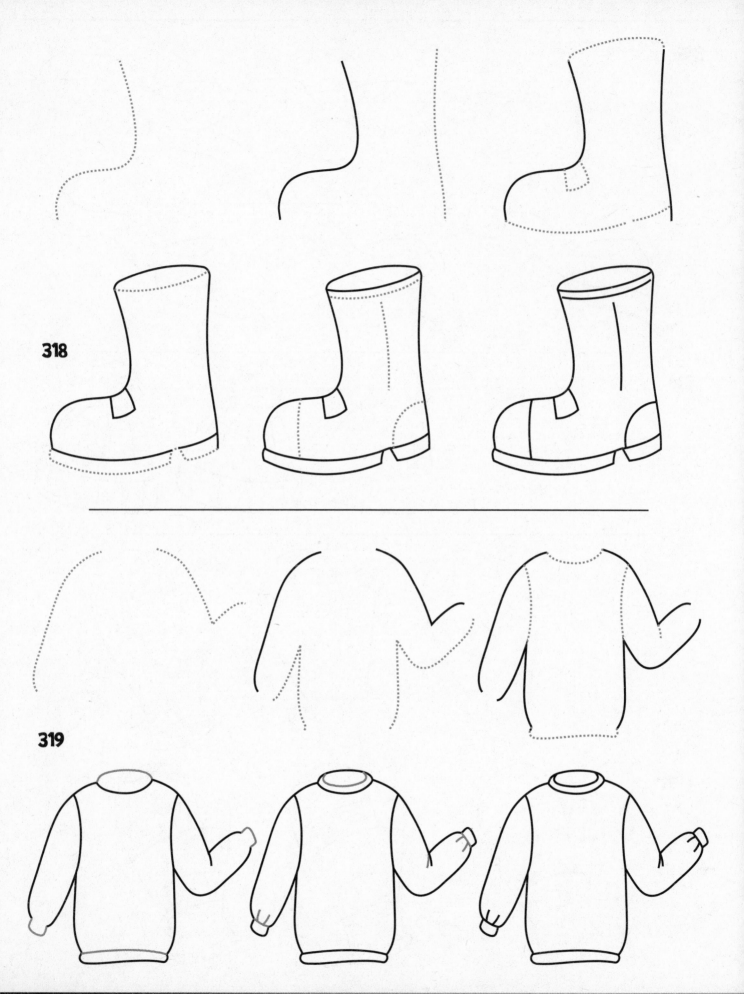

318

319

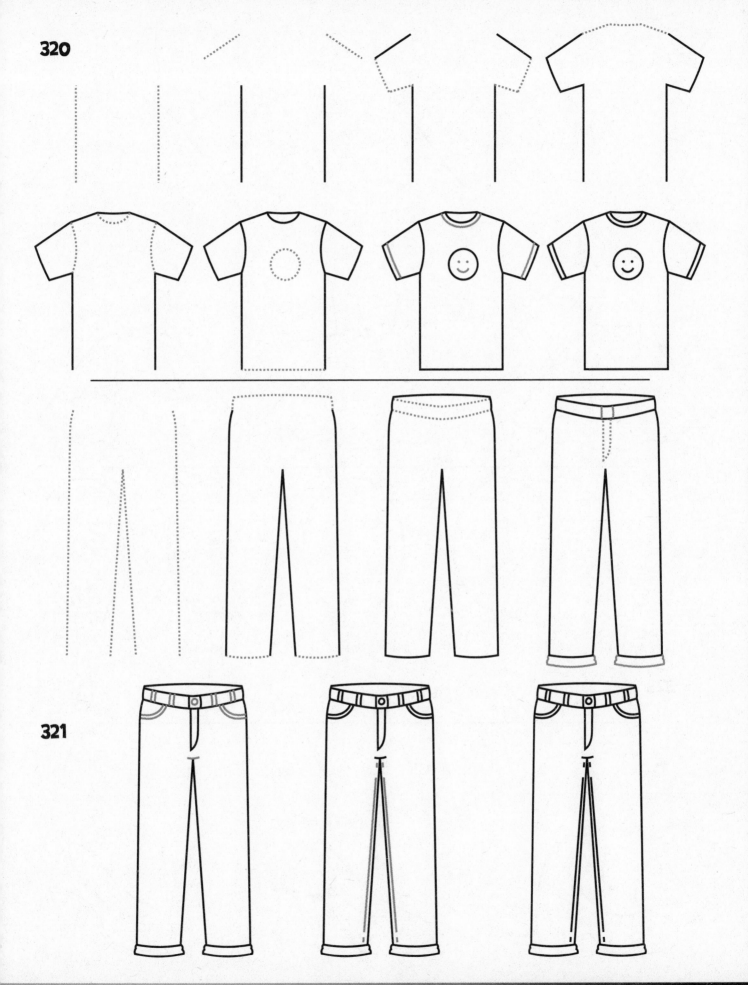

320

321

322

323

324

325

326

327

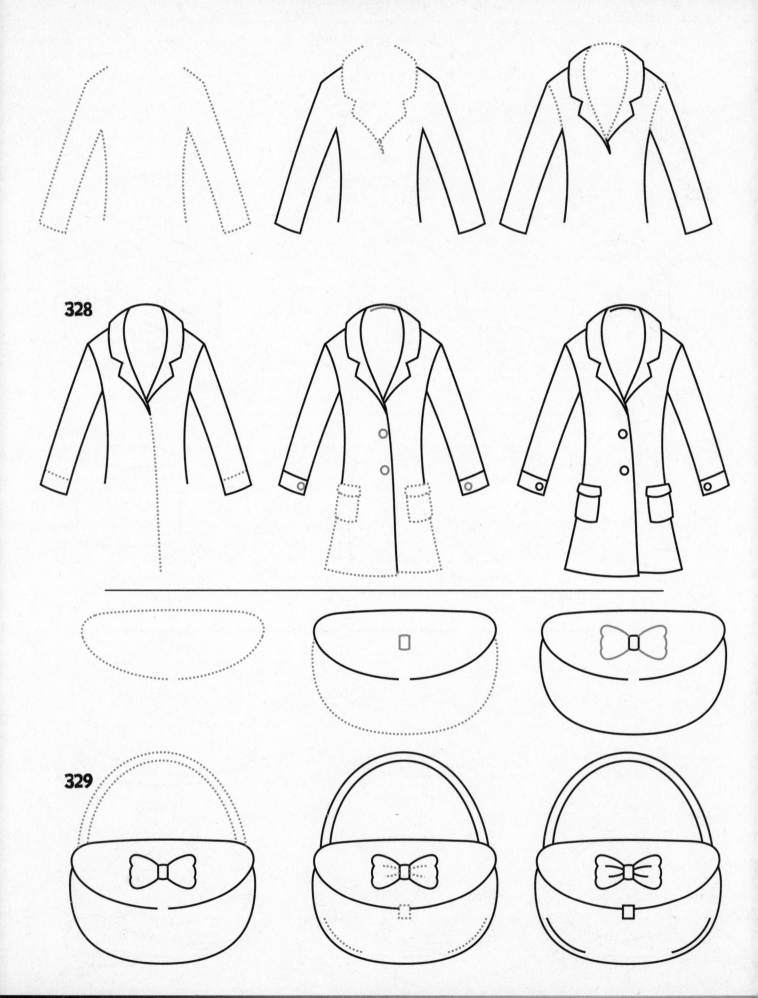

328

329

330

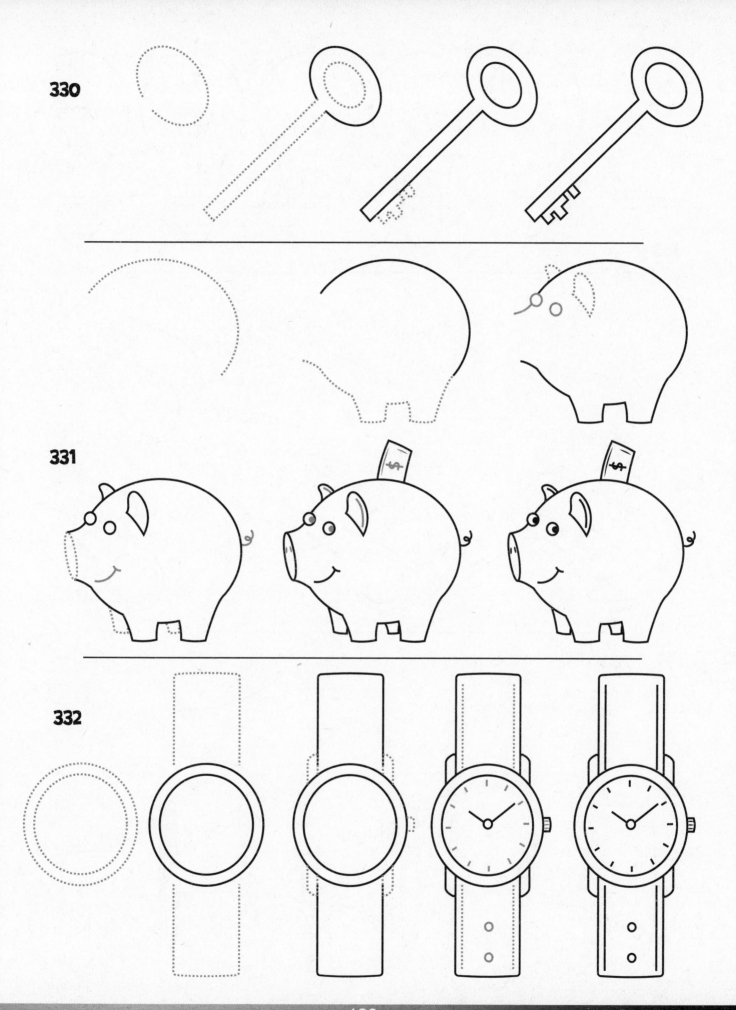

331

332

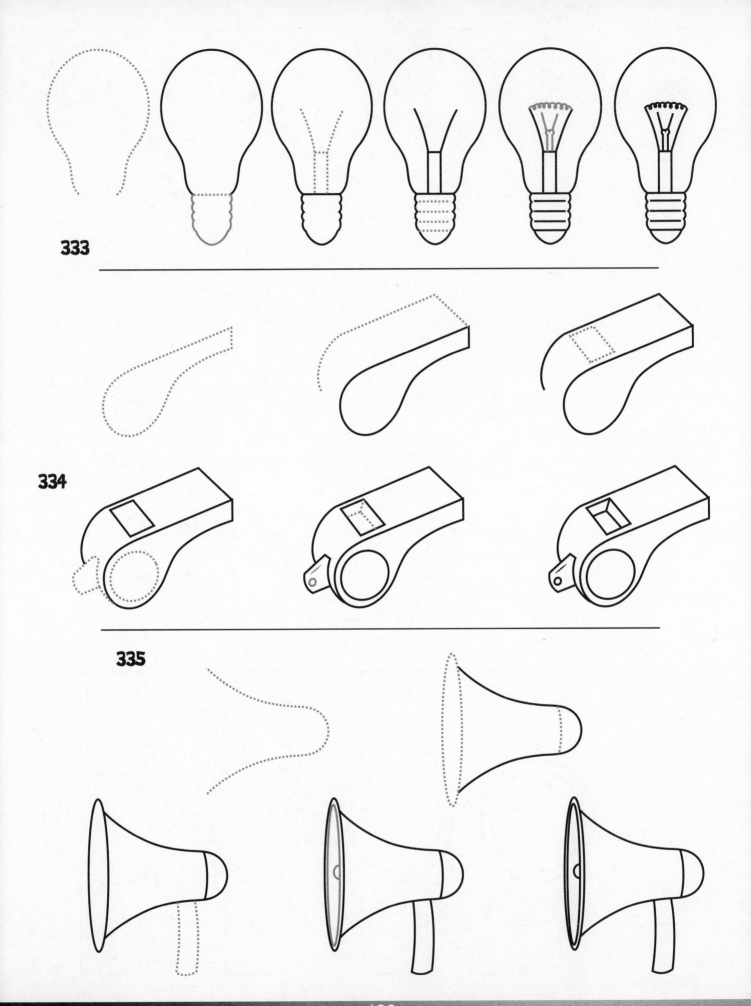

333

334

335

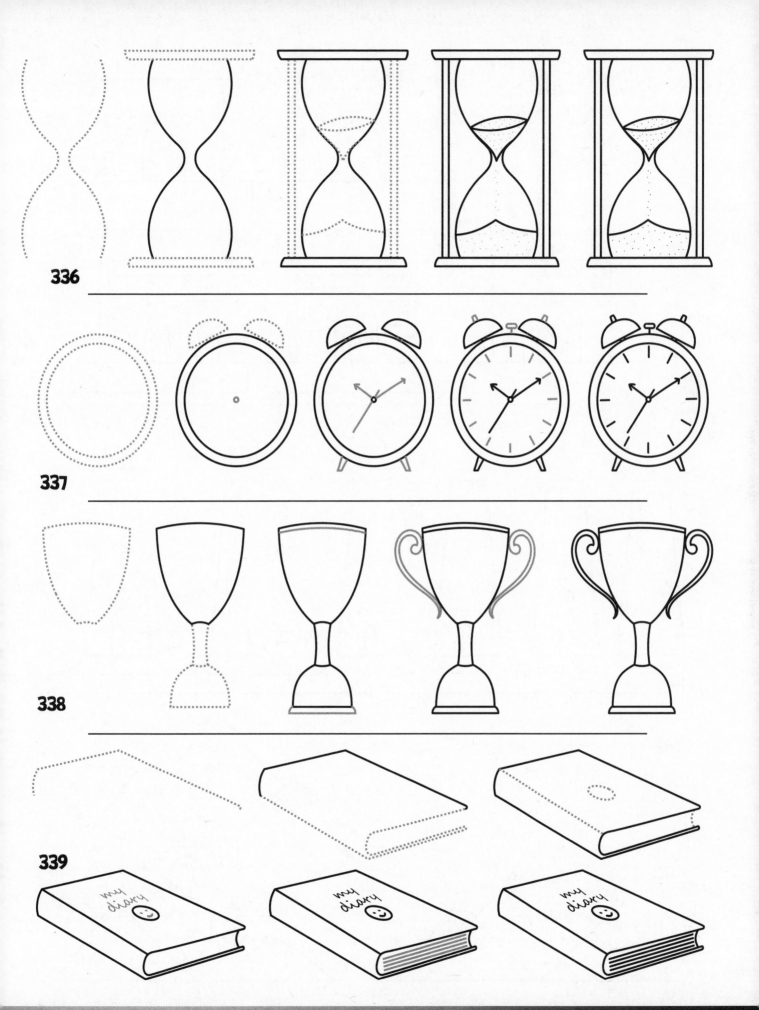

336

337

338

339

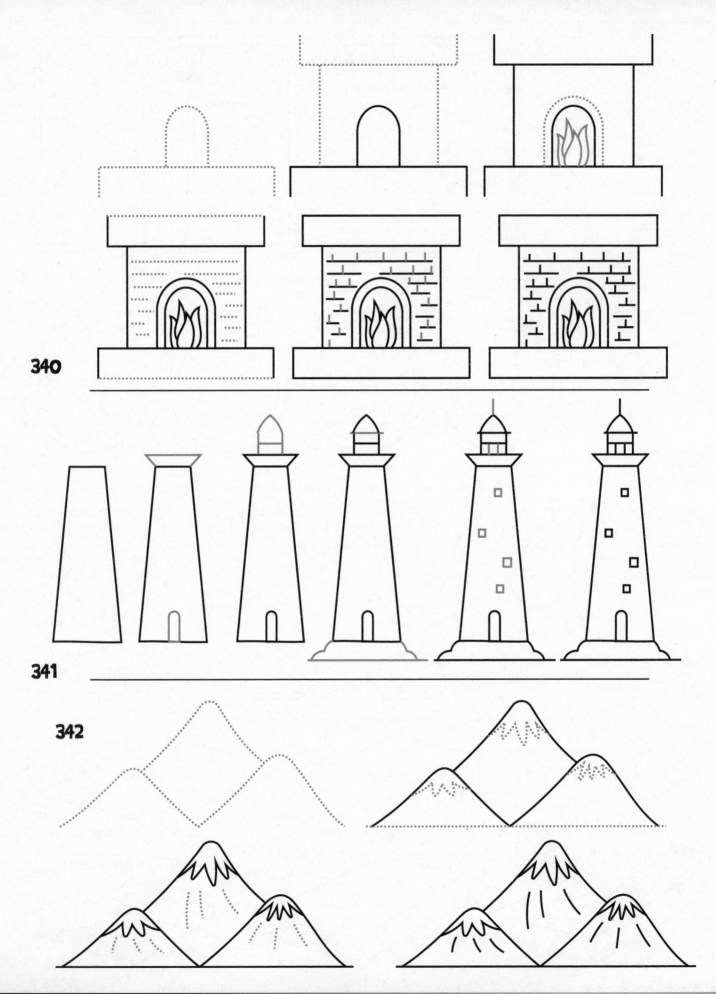

340

341

342

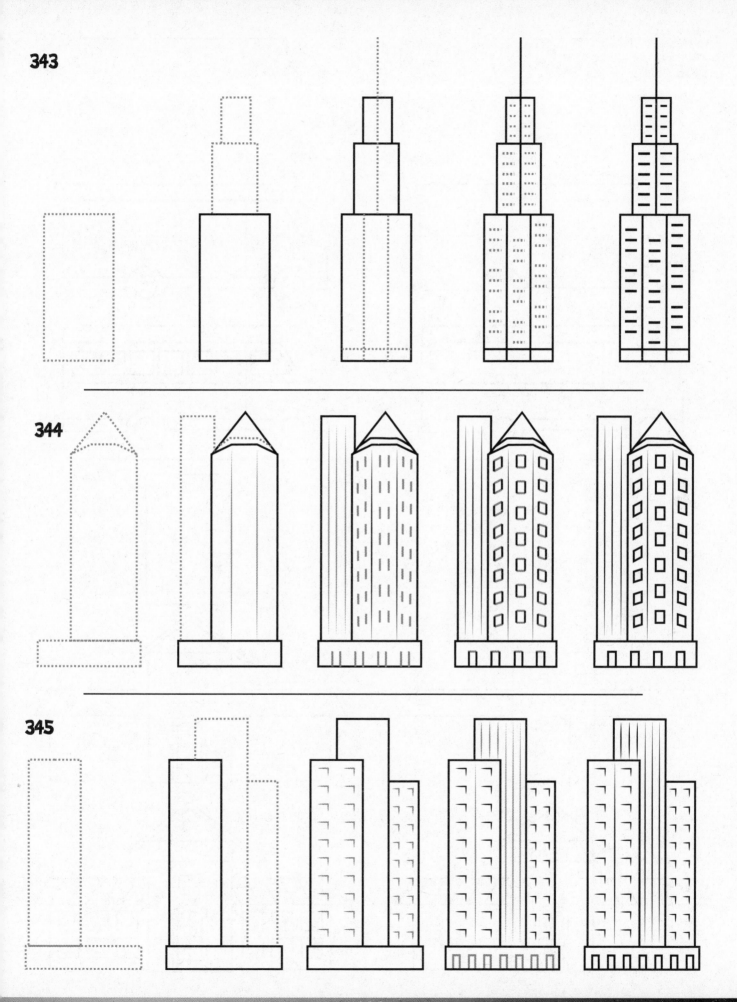

343

344

345

346

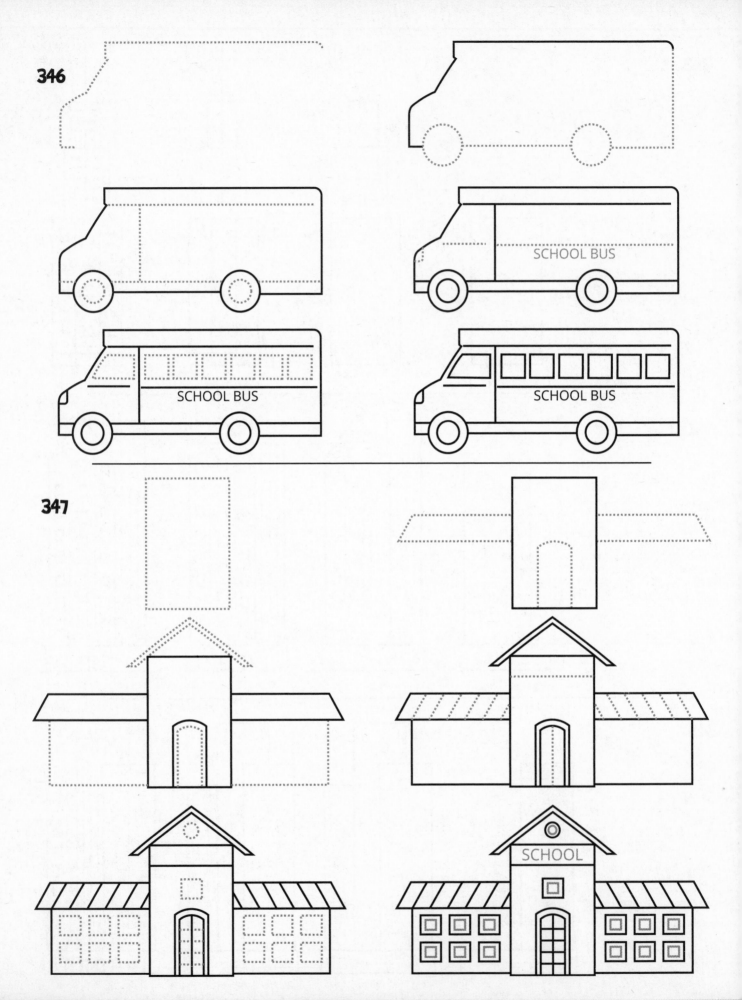

347

SCHOOL BUS

SCHOOL

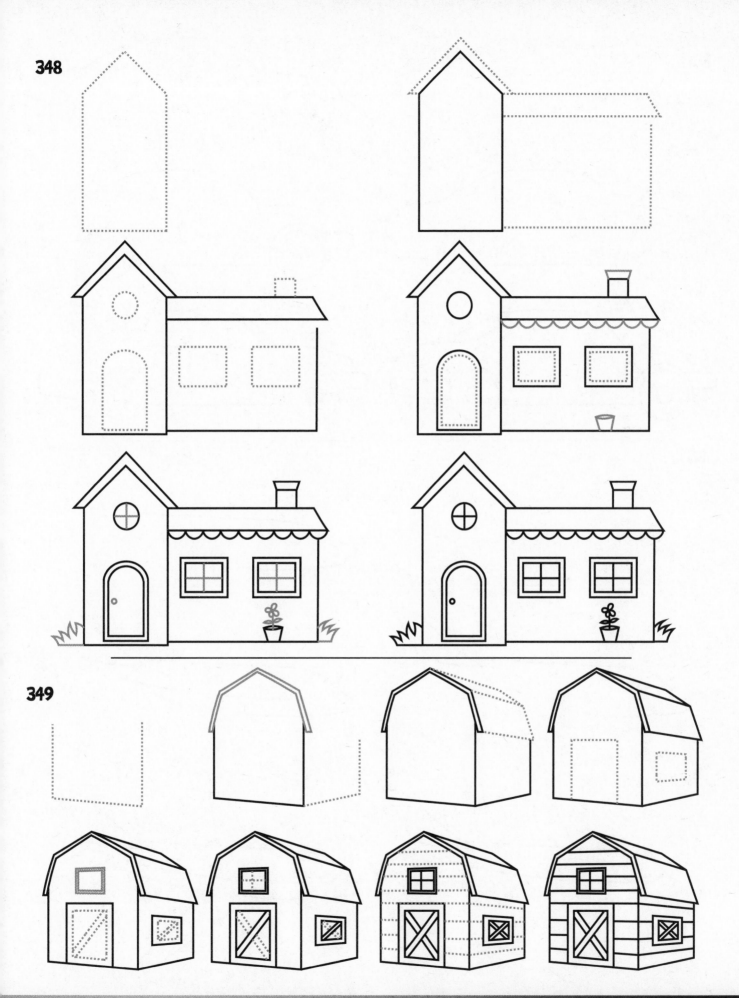

348

349

350

351

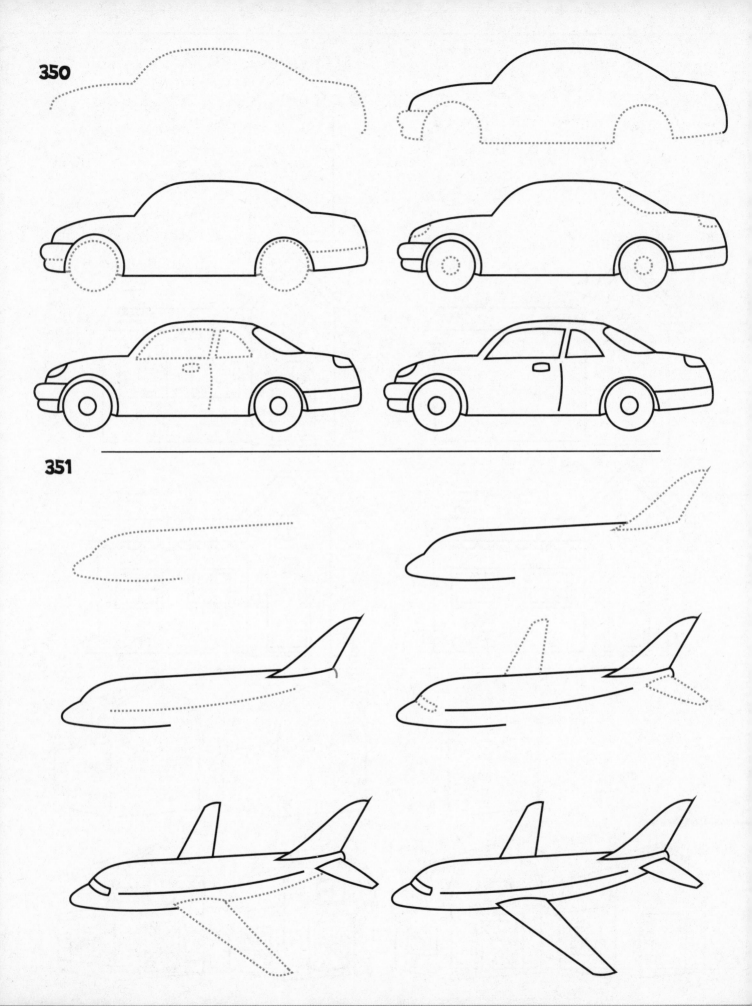

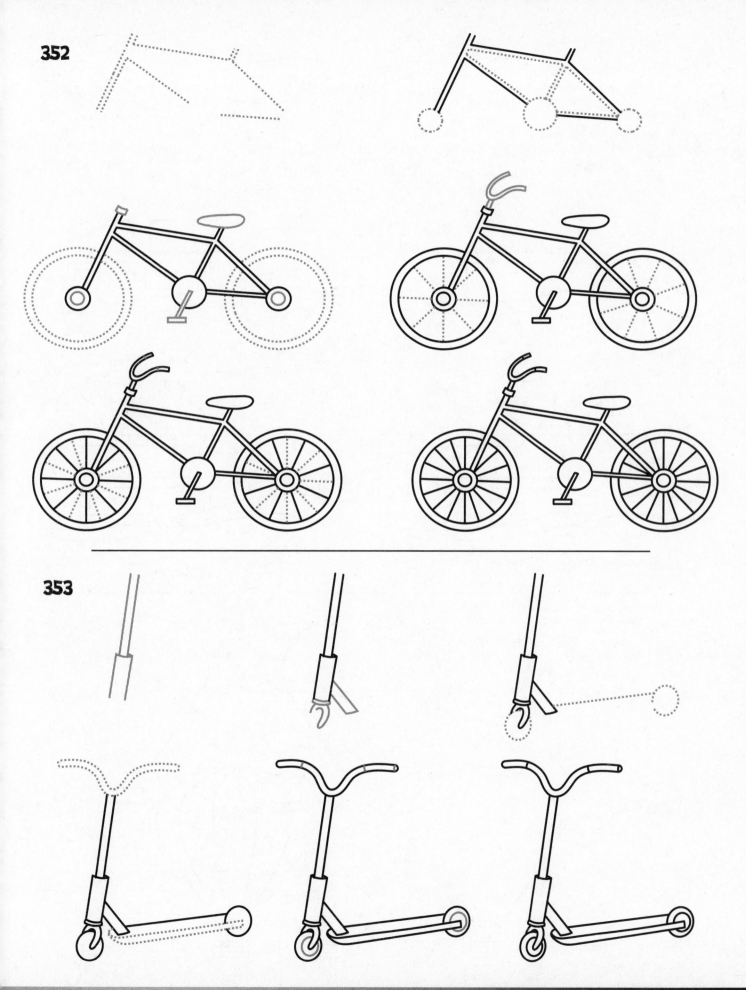

352

353

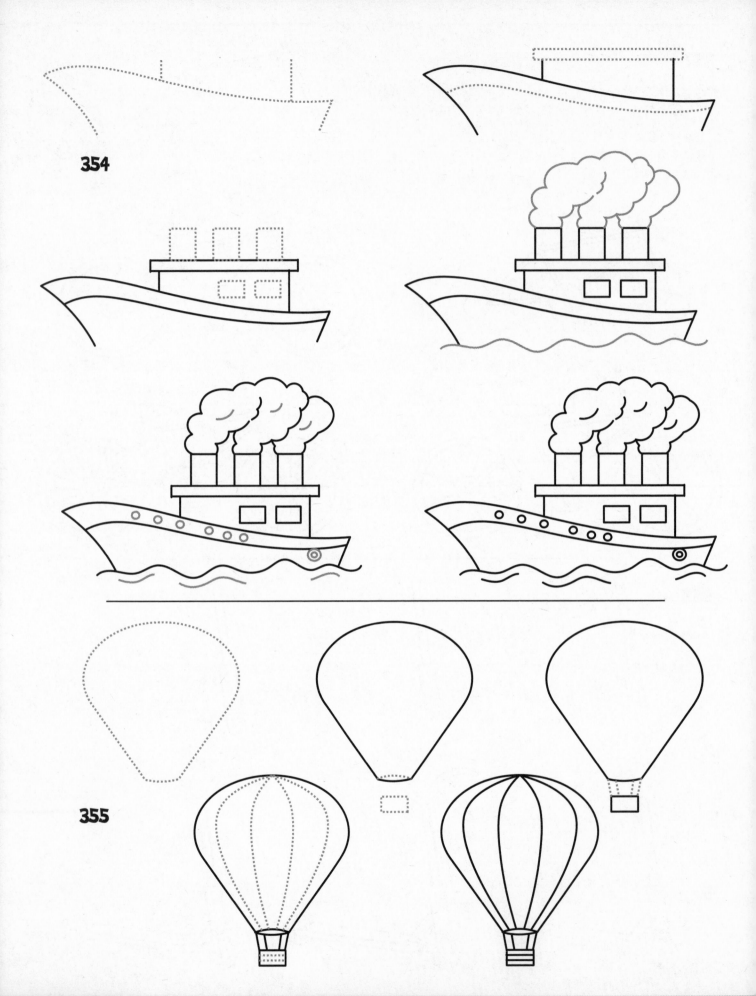

354

355

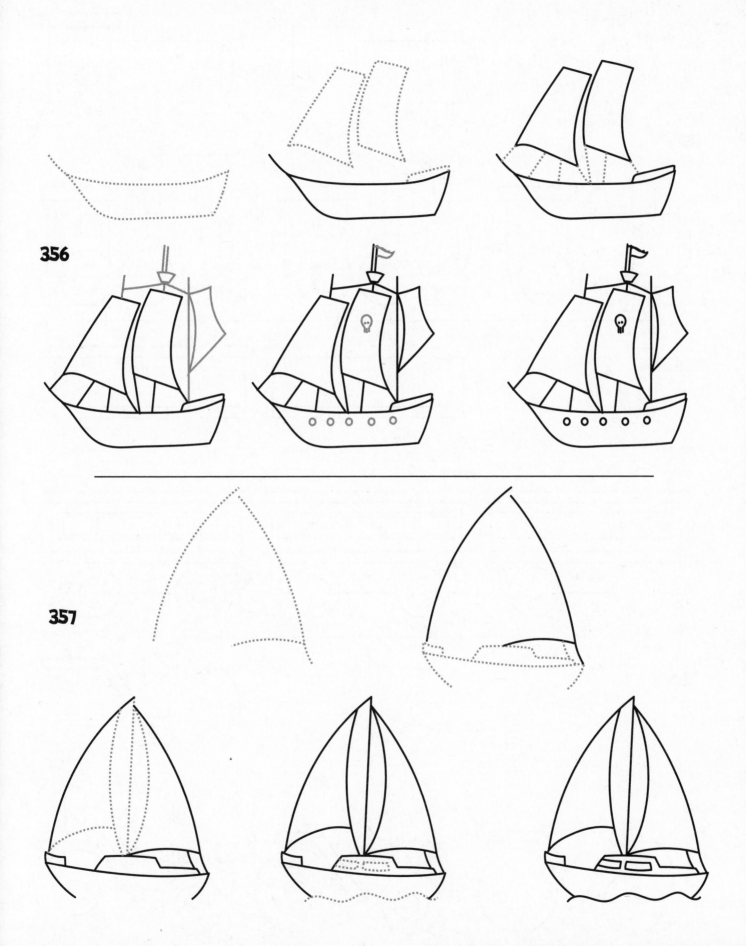

356

357

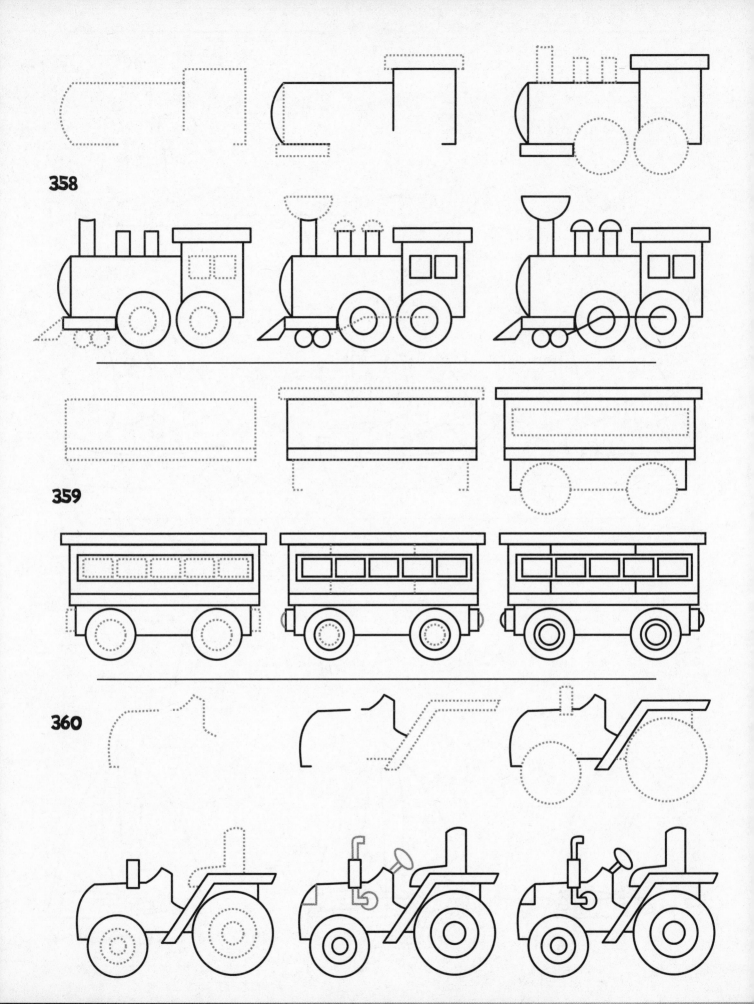

358

359

360

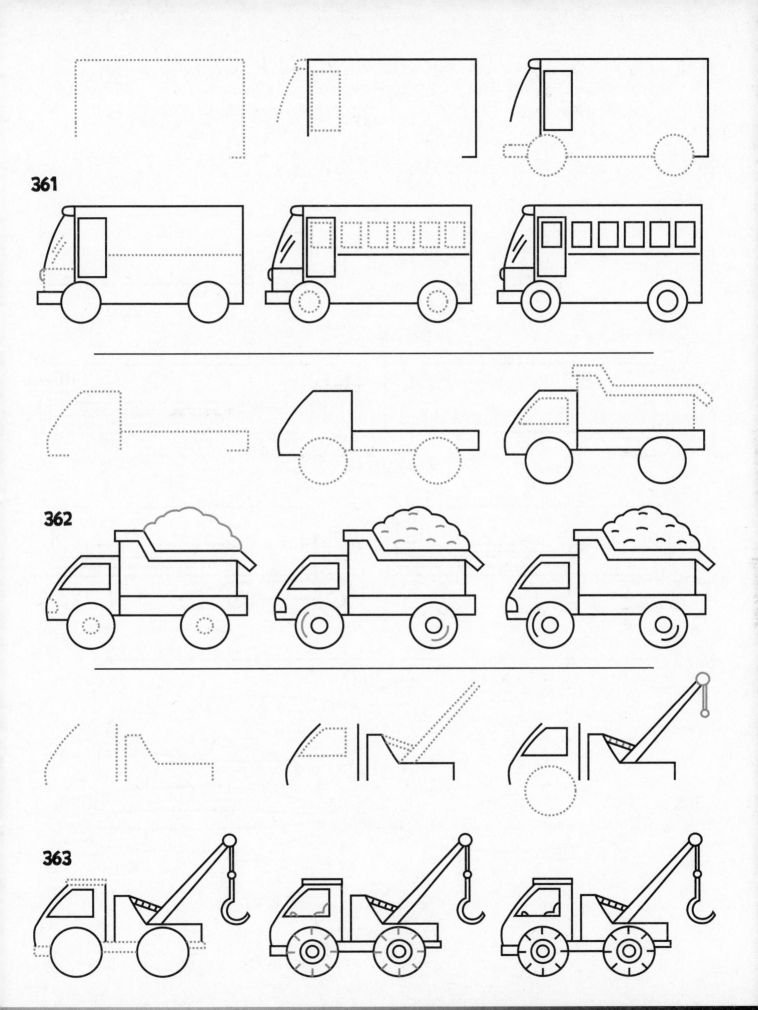

361

362

363

364

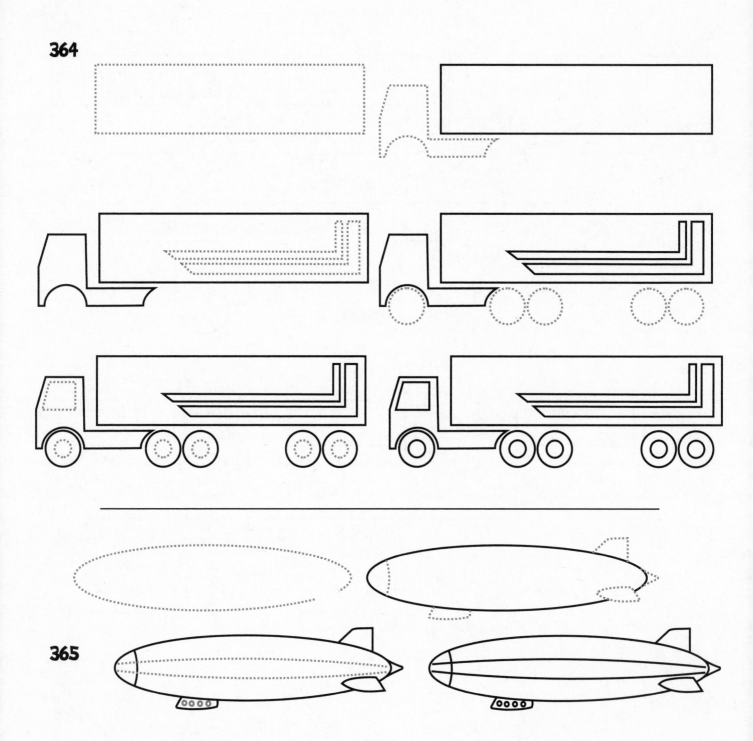

365

Woo! Jr. Kids' Activities is passionate about inspiring children to learn through imagination and FUN. That is why we have provided thousands of craft ideas, printables, and teacher resources to over 55 million people since 2008. We are on a mission to produce books that allow kids to build knowledge, express their talent, and grow into creative, compassionate human beings. Elementary education teachers, day care professionals, and parents have come to rely on Woo! Jr. for high quality, engaging, and innovative content that children LOVE. Our best-selling kids activity books have sold over 375,000 copies worldwide.

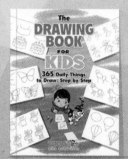

Tap into our free kids activity ideas at our website WooJr.com or by following us on social media: